High-Performance

SKATING
FOR HOCKEY

Steve Cady
Associate Athletic Director
Miami University

Vern Stenlund, EdD
Director of Program Development
Huron Hockey School

Human Kinetics

Library of Congress Cataloging-in-Publication Data

Cady, Steve, 1953-
    High-performance skating for hockey / Steve Cady, Vern Stenlund.
        p.   cm.
    ISBN 0-88011-773-7 (pbk.)
    1. Hockey--Training.   I. Stenlund, K. Vern.   II. Title.
  GV848.3.C33 1998   98-15931
  796.962'2--dc21   CIP

ISBN: 0-88011-773-7

Developmental Editor: Laura Casey Mast
Assistant Editor: Cynthia McEntire
Copyeditor: Bob Replinger
Proofreader: Erin Cler
Graphic Designer: Robert Reuther
Graphic Artist: Judy Henderson
Photo Editor: Boyd LaFoon
Cover Designer: Jack Davis
Photographer (cover): Tim DeFrisco
Photographer (interior): Tom Roberts
Illustrators: Kim Maxey, Jennifer Delmotte
Printer: V.G. Reed

Human Kinetics books are available at special discounts for bulk purchase. Special editions or book excerpts can also be created to specification. For details, contact the Special Sales Manager at Human Kinetics.

Printed in the United States of America   10 9 8 7 6 5 4 3 2 1

Human Kinetics
Web site: http://www.humankinetics.com/

United States: Human Kinetics
P.O. Box 5076
Champaign, IL 61825-5076
1-800-747-4457
e-mail: humank@hkusa.com

Canada: Human Kinetics
475 Devonshire Road, Unit 100
Windsor, ON N8Y 2L5
1-800-465-7301 (in Canada only)
e-mail: humank@hkcanada.com

Europe: Human Kinetics, P.O. Box IW14
Leeds LS16 6TR, United Kingdom
(44) 1132 781708
e-mail: humank@hkeurope.com

Australia: Human Kinetics
57A Price Avenue
Lower Mitcham, South Australia 5062
(088) 277 1555
e-mail: humank@hkaustralia.com

New Zealand: Human Kinetics
P.O. Box 105-231, Auckland 1
(09) 523 3462
e-mail: humank@hknewz.com

We dedicate this work to the following people:

To Sue, Matt, and Kevin Cady, thank you for your support and love through the years. Our family has always been my greatest blessing. I love you all.

To Lynne, Laura, Kara, Erik, and Tyler Stenlund, thank you for allowing me the time to complete this work. And special thanks for making Dad laugh through some difficult rewrites.

Contents

Drill Finder

The Drill Finder is a reference for quick identification of the various aspects of skating found in the drills and activities in this book. Although we have organized these drills within specific chapters that deal with a unique aspect of skating, in many cases you can use a drill to practice other skill areas or provide a greater challenge. In addition, although we may have introduced a drill as a forward-skating activity and identified it accordingly in the Drill Finder, players can attempt many of these drills skating either forward or backward. Finally, by identifying and understanding the many peripheral skills included in each drill, you may find it easier to organize efficient practices using a variety of themes.

Drill #	Drill	Forward	Backward	Starts	Stops	Turns	Pivots	Conditioning	Fun
1	One-Legged Glide	X							
2	Leg Loading	X							
3	Three-Count Recovery	X							
4	Railroad	X							
5	Sculling	X							
6	Frog Leaps	X						X	X
7	One-Legged Back Glide		X						
8	Backward Leg Load		X						
9	C-Cut Recovery		X						
10	Alternate C-Cuts		X						
11	C-Cut, Crossover Step Through		X						
12	Hourglass		X						
13	Duck Walk	X		X					
14	Three-Stick Drill	X		X					
15	Falling Stick	X		X					X
16	Sideways Walk	X		X					
17	Coach's Command	X		X					
18	Zigzag	X			X				
19	Left- and Right-Foot Stops	X			X				
20	Skiing	X			X		X		
21	Partner Pull	X	X	X					X
22	360-Degree Turns	X				X			
23	Figure 8	X				X			
24	Slalom	X				X			X
25	Airplane	X				X			
26	Clock Drill	X				X			
27	Partner Circle	X				X		X	X
28	Sculling Circle	X				X			
29	Four-Step Command	X					X		
30	Alternating 180s	X					X		
31	Four Corners	X					X		
32	Russian Kip, Forward and Backward	X						X	X
33	Shoot the Duck	X						X	X
34	Swedish C-Cut, Backward	X						X	X
35	Russian Walk	X						X	X
36	Jump Rope	X						X	X
37	Power Pulls	X						X	X

Foreword

Hockey is quickly becoming one of the most popular sports in the world, and why not? It has elements that appeal to many sports spectators and participants—intense physical play, athleticism, strategy, and speed. The last point is key as hockey has become a game in which quickness and flat-out speed determine who will make it to the top level.

In *High-Performance Skating for Hockey*, authors Cady and Stenlund give players everything they need to become the best skaters possible. Each chapter provides sound coaching and practice ideas that will improve skating ability and acceleration by building confidence and control. At elite levels of hockey, one second translates into 20 to 30 feet of distance at top speed. If the secrets in this book teach you how to trim just one-tenth of a second from a turn, pivot, start, or stop, you could gain a two- or three-foot advantage while playing the game. That advantage might be the difference between winning and losing.

This book contains the most current and helpful skating information I've ever seen. I know that once you read it and understand the concepts put forward by these two authors, your skating performance will improve dramatically.

Ron Mason
Head Coach, Michigan State University

Acknowledgments

The authors wish to express their appreciation for Tom Roberts, Doug Fink, Roger Francisco, Andrea Whitesell, Laura Casey Mast, Ted Miller, and all the great people at Human Kinetics; Matt and Kevin Cady, and Justin Otto at Huron Hockey School who posed for the photos; the arena staff at Miami University; those who helped with the photo shoot in Oxford; Mark Hughes and all colleagues at Easton Hockey; and Chad Clark and all colleagues at Rival and especially Huron Hockey, Inc.

Key to Diagrams

 Coach or leader

X   Player

 Cone or pylon

Net or goal

 Player skating/direction of travel

 Skate

Blade mark on ice

Introduction: Getting a Split-Second Edge on Ice

Why do players such as Paul Coffey, Mark Messier, Paul Kariya, and Joe Sakic appear to skate so effortlessly during a hockey game? Do these and other professional players possess secrets that give them a split-second edge in their sport, or do their natural athletic gifts make them stand out as world-class skaters and players? While no one can answer these questions definitively, we do know that hockey continues to evolve into a high-tempo, skills-based activity enjoyed by enthusiasts worldwide.

At its highest levels, hockey requires players of great athleticism, courage, and skill if they intend to make a career of the sport. Yet of all the skills required to excel in hockey, none is more important than sound skating technique, the very foundation of the game. Aspiring players must be ready to improve their skating mechanics to keep pace with the competition. Contemporary hockey players, including the notable superstars just mentioned, have realized that they must first understand skating, then apply it, and finally practice it to ensure maximum enjoyment and advancement in the game.

This book is designed to help you—player, coach, or skating instructor—master skating skills in hockey. By first understanding the principles behind skating mechanics you will be in a better position to master the skills and drills presented in these pages, skills and drills that are time tested and proven to be effective in developing better skaters. Mastering these skills will permit you to command the flow of a game by controlling one of the most vital components of the game—skating!

Just how important is skating to the game of hockey? Important enough that Huron Hockey School devotes half of each clinic day to explaining and refining skating mechanics. Coaches and players who move into other areas of the game before having a clear understanding of skating undermine their potential for high-level, long-term success. The Golden Bear, golfing legend Jack Nicklaus, once wrote that he could not move into the elite levels of golf until he learned how to self-correct on the course when things began to go wrong. Like the golfer who can successfully analyze a poor shot during competition and effect important changes to his or her swing, hockey players must be able to understand and perform important aspects of skating before advancing into additional skill areas.

As you move forward in this book and attempt some of the drills, you might find yourself asking, "What does this activity have to do with hockey?" Do not be fooled simply because a drill does not focus on scoring goals or checking an opponent. On the surface many of the activities may not seem to be hockey related, but what you will be doing is reinforcing key principles through practice, principles that will show you how your upper- and lower-body areas work together. In the process you will come to appreciate proper balance and balance points unique to your body, which will positively affect your skating efficiency and movement.

The player who appreciates and develops proper mechanics conserves energy. The athlete who uses less energy during a game will have an advantage late in the contest that could be the difference between victory and defeat. Former Chicago Blackhawk 50-goal scorer Al Secord spent many summers with Huron instructors identifying weaknesses and then correcting them. At one point in his career he suffered an abdominal injury and, after resting until fully healed, returned to the lineup with a clean bill of health. His game performance, however, had slipped dramatically. Upon reviewing videotapes of Al in game situations, an instructor determined that he had altered his skating position to protect the abdominal area. Al made the necessary changes in his skating mechanics, and his game again shifted into high gear. Many other pro players have confirmed what we already knew, namely, that they often do not truly understand the importance of skating until their playing days are through. One of our objectives in writing this book is to make sure that doesn't happen to you.

The information in this book applies to all levels of play—from the youngest beginner to the most experienced NHL all-star. Ted Sator, a master Huron teacher and former NHL head coach, notes that proper skating mechanics change little from peewee to pro; only the explanations become more sophisticated. The principles remain constant, but the drilling to reinforce these principles becomes more diverse and varied. Sometimes, coaches will lose sight of the broad context in describing skating mechanics, leaving players confused as to purpose or meaning. *High-Performance Skating for Hockey* is intended to simplify skating so that all participants can improve and enjoy hockey to the fullest through easily understood explanations and drilling techniques.

This book, however, provides more than just drills. We have also included valuable tips and ideas for each activity that will help players and coaches reduce the time required to master a skill. In assembling the drills for this book we gave special attention to providing activities that beginners will find doable almost immediately, allowing players at any level to achieve a measure of success. As players' skills increase, so too will their ability to perform the activities at a faster pace using less space. They will know their skating skills have improved because they will be able to see and feel the results.

As you look at the individual drills in this book, pay special attention to the Key Points section of each activity. There you will find many helpful ideas and suggestions to help you perfect the drills. Years of teaching and coaching experience have gone into developing these activities, and the comments that accompany them reflect the approaches of many coaches who have reached the professional level. Their advice will serve you well as you continue along the road to mastery.

How the Book Is Organized

The drills have been assembled with some specific objectives in mind. The first one is basic but especially important. Rather than combining drills from all phases of hockey, this book looks at one major aspect of play, namely, moving toward a high level of skill in skating. We did this so the reader would avoid one of the pitfalls that many coaches and players encounter when they buy a book or video filled with new drills. Armed with a wealth of new information they go home ready to conquer the world. What they inevitably realize is that many instructional materials are too complicated and do not provide players with appropriate drills for their skill level. Often the result is confusion and frustration for everyone involved.

Second, this book presents a level of progression from simple activities at the beginning of each chapter to more difficult drills at the end of each chapter. On a larger scale, the same philosophy applies, with each succeeding chapter of the book offering more challenging activities. In providing this progression, a wide range of players and coaches will find material presented here practical and useful.

Third, some chapters have specific sequences of drills that build upon one another. Working through these sequences will allow players to understand more clearly the objectives of the drills and master the skills more quickly. We have included sample practice plans so coaches and players can see how they can integrate drills into practice sessions. To make practice planning easier, use the Drill Finder section to identify other aspects of play incorporated by specific drills.

Finally, you will notice that the drills rarely require extra equipment or substantial setup time. Most require only a pair of skates and some ice. As a result, you can do the drills with little waste of time and effort. You spend valuable ice time doing the activities, not discussing them.

If you really want to gain that split-second edge over your opponent, *High-Performance Skating for Hockey* is the book for you. We hope that by using this resource players will be able to teach themselves the finer points of skating.

A final note: no helmets were worn during the photo shoot for this book. The photo shoot took place under very controlled conditions during which no intense skating took place or physical contact was made between players. Human Kinetics and Huron Hockey, Inc. strongly advise players to always wear head and face protection during any practice or game situation.

Good luck and good skating!

Key Terms and Definitions

Basic words and terms associated with skating are described and defined here to ensure your understanding of important concepts used in this book. If you do not understand a word or phrase somewhere in a later chapter, please refer to this section for clarification.

Arms—Do not underestimate the importance of the arms in overall skating efficiency. Just as in walking or running, each arm moves in combination with the opposite leg. Players find this a natural motion as they get comfortable on the ice. The arms should extend toward an imaginary midpoint line in the body, but not beyond, during normal skating conditions (figure a). This permits proper stick positioning when a puck arrives and guarantees that the player will not swing the arms in a counterproductive fashion.

Ball of the foot—The area of the foot directly behind the toes.

Edges—The blades of skates comprise three main areas, commonly referred to as skate edges. These include the inside edge, outside edge, and flats of the blade. The inside edge is used primarily to push off while striding and plays a critical part in stopping and turning (figure b). The outside edge is emphasized primarily while turning, while the flats or bottom portion of the blade is the key element used to glide along the ice surface while the skater applies equal pressure to the inside and outside edges of the blade (figures c and d). Being able to control the three areas of the skate blade is critical to effective skating.

Extension—Commonly used to describe proper mechanics of the stride leg, as in "full extension" in which the leg is com-

(a) Correct and incorrect arm positions

pletely straight after a stride action occurs. To obtain maximum efficiency, it is important to begin extension from the hip through the knee and ankle joint when completing a stride.

Glide phase—When both edges of the support-leg skate glide along the ice close to the midline of the body (figure e).

Head and neck area—The location of this area requires no definition; however, an explanation is required about how important this region of the body is to skating. Players must get in the rhythm of keeping the head up. The eyes should be looking forward rather than down at the ice surface or at the puck on the stick. This is especially important to the skater when confronted by a six-foot-four, 220-pound defenseman who is about to deliver a body check. Keeping the head down normally suggests that the knees will be straight, which is incorrect form. Also, by looking out the player can quickly

(b) Inside edge of skate blade

(c) Outside edge of skate blade

(d) Flat edge of skate blade

(e) The glide phase

determine whether to change direction. The head and neck play a key part in this skating technique. By turning the head quickly in the intended direction, the skater can execute the turn with greater speed because the rest of the body will follow the lead. Turning by leading with the stick, for example, is not as fast. Players should keep the eyes looking out and be ready to snap the head in another direction to change their skating course (figure f).

Heel kick—Refers to the back part of the skate, the heel, pointing upward while the toe of the skate is facing the ice surface. Players should avoid excessive heel kick because it wastes time and restricts overall skating speed by increasing recovery time after each stride.

Loading—In skating, loading up generally refers to bending the knee joint close to a 90-degree angle. Loading allows the big muscle groups of the legs, such as the quadriceps (located on

(f) Correct head and neck alignment with eyes looking up

the front of the upper portion of the leg) and the hamstrings (located on the back portion of the upper leg) to generate maximum strength for skating.

Midbody region—The waist or trunk area is a key for skating because of the proximity of abdominal muscles. These muscle groups must be strong to support sound skating technique. The ideal biomechanic alignment would see the waist bent enough to allow a straight vertical line to be drawn through the chin, knee, and toe (figure g).

Proper balance—The optimal positions for alignment of upper- and lower-body segments to allow maximum support and control for executing any hockey-related skill (figure h).

Pitching hay—Occurs when the arms cross the midline of the body when a player has two hands on the stick shaft. The result will be that the player will raise the stick side to side in

(g) Correct midbody posture

(h) Proper balance

the air at 90 degrees to the line of travel, reducing overall skating speed.

Recovery phase—Refers to retrieving the stride leg back under the body once a skater has completed a single pushing action.

Shoulders and chest area—This region of the body is key to maintaining a strong skating technique, which is especially important for turning. By keeping the chest out and the shoulders level, the entire upper carriage remains stable, whether in a straight-line skating pattern or in a tight turn. It makes sense to keep the chest and shoulders square to the intended direction so that the target area is observable (figure i).

Stride leg and stride phase—This is the action leg in skating, the one that pushes back and away from the body to create motion.

(i) Correct shoulder and chest alignment

Support leg—This is the leg located directly under the body and in line with the chin, acting to support most of the body weight during skating sequences. The skater should bend the leg close to 90 degrees so that the big leg muscles will produce maximal strength in the next push. The player should distribute weight over the ball of the foot of the support leg (figure j).

(j) Correct position of the support leg

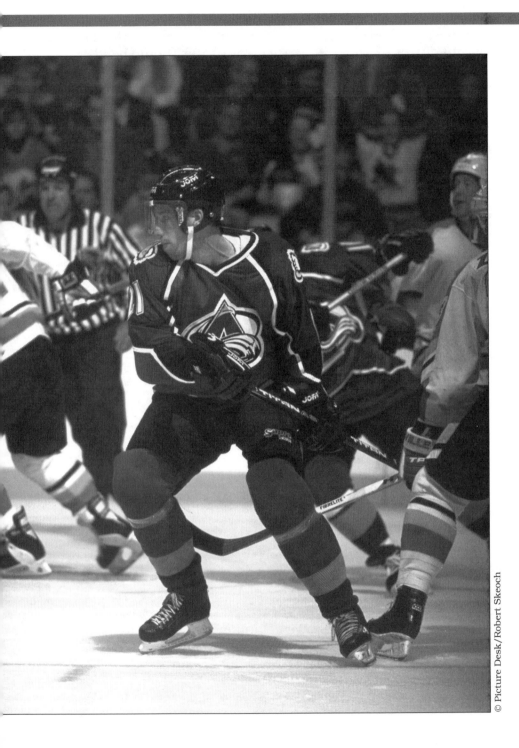

1

Skating Essentials

Skating is the most fundamental aspect of ice hockey. Without proper skating technique, skill development in other areas of the game becomes increasingly difficult. Huron hockey instructors have traveled all over the world to gather data and insights while developing a philosophy of teaching sound principles of skating. From studying the leg and foot movements of Olympic sprinters to pioneering the use of videotape in hockey to assess skating technique, Huron personnel have labored to develop a comprehensive curriculum for promoting proper skating mechanics. Like many European coaches, we believe that certain basic principles exist in proper skating execution for all skaters—hockey players, figure skaters, speed skaters, or simply people who enjoy the recreational aspects of skating. We have come to a simple yet powerful conclusion based on our research, namely that

Skating is ultimately an alternating,
one-legged balancing act.

With this as our basic premise, the information that follows in these pages is an attempt to make this balancing act work effectively and efficiently. We examine each major aspect of skating, emphasizing the development of proper posture to improve balance. The main objective of this book is to provide information to make this balancing act work for you. More important, we want you to be able to assess what is happening

1

with your unique balancing act as a first step toward skating improvement.

In this chapter we will examine some essential components that you must possess if you intend to improve your skating. These points are the foundation. Everything that follows assumes that you have read and understand these concepts. As you progress through the drills and activities it may be useful to check back to this chapter to ensure that you have learned the essential components. You will more quickly and easily advance your skating skills if you remember the ideas from this section. The first of these essentials centers on the skate itself because this piece of equipment will have a significant impact on skating proficiency.

Essential #1
Get the Right Skates for You

It is difficult, especially for newer players, to execute the activities in this book properly if their skates are not right for them. You might be asking yourself, "What exactly is the right skate for me?" Skaters should keep several points in mind when choosing a new pair of skates. For example, make sure that the boot fits properly with the foot being neither too loose nor too cramped once the laces are tied. Do not purchase skates that are too large with the idea of having a player use the same skates over several seasons, thus saving money. It is better to buy a lower-priced or used skate that fits properly than an oversized, big-ticket item that will deter the player from learning proper mechanics.

Sizing is just one element that players should consider when buying new skates. Many kinds of skates are on the market today, providing consumers with a variety of choices. Included in this opening section is a chart that identifies key elements to look for when buying, breaking in, and maintaining your skates.

Skate Key

Skate Fit

- Make sure you do not purchase skates that are too large. Wearing skates that are too large will impede your ability to execute skating skills. Your big toe should be barely touching the front portion of the toe cap. Too much space here is not beneficial to skating.
- Ensure that your heels rest flat in the back of each skate.
- You should have skates that offer adequate ankle support. Younger skaters especially should choose skates with ample support because their lack of strength and balance will contribute to excessive ankle roll toward the inside edges.

Skate Composition

Boot

- Molded plastic versus leather or stitched
- Newer boot materials
- Depending on the materials that make up the skate, you will feel very stiff in the boot or more flexible around the ankle area. This is a matter of personal choice.
- Newer materials have a unique feel.

Blades

- Different types of steel composition
- Rockered versus nonrockered
- Make sure the blades are made of high-grade steel that will withstand rust (check the manufacturer's specs).
- Rocker of the blade refers to the amount of blade curvature from toe to heel. This again is a matter of personal choice and skating style.

Tongue

- Standard types
- Foam-injection molding
- Some manufacturers offer unique products such as pump-up or form-fitting tongues in certain skate models.
- The length is variable with some of the longer ones adding additional protection between the shin pad and top of skate boot.

Skate Maintenance

- Lace the boot correctly.
- Do not overtighten near the toe area. This can impede blood flow, which will cause cold and uncomfortable feet.
- When replacing laces buy the proper length. Avoid having excess length that could unravel during play or drag along the ice.
- Use every eyelet in the boot.
- Simply stated, skate in them as much as you can!
- Do not put them in the oven to soften the leather.
- Do not submerge in hot water.
- Do not wait for fall tryouts before trying your new skates. It could be a painful experience.
- Get into a system of maintaining your skates.
- Remember not to walk on surfaces such as cement with exposed skate blades. If you must walk over this type of surface to get to the ice, use skate guards.
- Carry a towel with you to the rink and get into the routine of thoroughly wiping excess moisture from the blades after each use. Give the boot area a quick cleaning as well.
- Sharpen your skate blades as the need arises or if a major nick develops in the blade.
- It's a good idea to keep a small sharpening stone in your hockey bag. Often you won't need to have both

blades sharpened. A quick pass with a stone will smooth the edges of your blades as much as you need.

Skate Cost

- If you are a young, beginning player there is no need to get the top-of-the-line skate because you will probably outgrow them in a year. Proper fit with appropriate support is critical.
- Once you have made a commitment to play, especially as you move into higher levels, then a higher-grade boot might be more applicable. Once-a-week players probably will never need the top-of-the-line skates.
- Several skate companies have been in existence for many years and have well-established reputations. If you choose to buy top-end skates, compare pricing and quality because they vary across manufacturers.
- There is an ever increasing market for used skates and other hockey-related equipment. Many sports stores now have sections specific to these needs.
- Your hockey association might offer a swap market where parents can upgrade to bigger and better used skates at a fraction of the cost of new ones.

Essential #2
Key on Proper Posture and Balance Points for Proper Skating

No two hockey players skate alike. Each skater develops a style over time, a style that often results from a series of corrections made to overcome some form of skating problem. Sometimes those problems originate with posture. In the National Hockey League many players are identified as being graceful, almost effortless skaters who get big returns on the efforts they expend. Players such as Mike Gartner, Sergei Fedorov, and Pavel Bure have established reputations as fine skaters who possess beautiful technique. All demonstrate proper posture while skating, which affects areas such as balance and speed.

But perhaps the best role model in recent years has been Paul Coffey, the future Hall of Fame defenseman, who seems to float on air once in motion. If you examine Coffey's skating posture you will learn some important clues to becoming an elite skater. We define proper posture as being made up of the following characteristics for ice skaters:

- Bent knees and ankles

- Slight forward lean at the waist

- Eyes looking forward, not down (sometimes referred to as having the head up)

- Proper alignment of upper and lower body:
  - front view: toe, knee, and chin aligned
  - side view: ankle, knee, hip, shoulder, and head aligned

- Proper weight distribution over skates on the balls of the feet

Picture in your mind a fluid skater like Paul Coffey, and you will see that he incorporates all these mechanics into his skating (figure 1.1). It is worth noting that Coffey's father realized early in his son's hockey development the importance of efficient skating. While many of his friends were taking time off, especially during the summer months, Paul was involved in skating lessons. Fans today look at Coffey and express amazement at this "naturally gifted skater," but Paul spent years learning the lessons of skating through proper practice and meaningful reinforcement.

We will examine the key characteristics associated with proper skating technique in detail in different sections of this book. For the time being it is reasonable to suggest that skaters who consistently fall on the ice, appear to use more energy than required, or cannot advance beyond a specific point of proficiency may be the victims of poor skating posture.

Figure 1.1   Paul Coffey in action

Essential #3
Develop Lower-Body Strength to Improve Technique

Efficient skating also requires considerable strength. Specifically, the big muscles located in the legs and the various muscle groups within the midbody region must be strong to provide the necessary foundation for fluid skating motion. You might have perfect posture and understand all the proper biomechanics of skating yet find that you are unable to skate efficiently over an extended time. Working to develop strength in the mid- to lower-body areas will allow you to combine style and substance during any competition.

Often we see younger participants in hockey having trouble with skating due simply to a lack of leg strength. This is especially true for players who are larger than average in height and weight for their age group. This is why smaller, lighter players often have an advantage in skating early in the developmental process. This has little to do with bigger players going through a clumsy stage; rather, it has to do with strength, or a lack of it! Several on- and off-ice activities are specifically included in this book to assist players in developing the strength to ensure proper skating technique.

Essential #4
Get Loose to Get Better

As in any sport that requires consistent improvement in any skill area, learning to skate is more easily accomplished by those who are physically prepared to meet the skill challenge. We recommend that you take the time, both on and off the ice, to prepare the specific muscle groups that you will use in skating. You can do this by using a well-conceived warm-up regimen that will develop greater flexibility and muscle receptiveness to ice-skating drills. Included in this section are some simple warm-up activities that will prepare you for your day's work on ice. Remember that there are no shortcuts to mastering sound skating technique, so don't forget to get ready with a few warm-up exercises.

Always stretch before and after practice. The stretches illustrated in the following pages represent a sound cross-section of muscle-specific warm-up activities. Other similar drills may be incorporated in your stretching routine. A simple routine will prepare the body for action while greatly reducing your risk of injury during play. Many coaches prefer to have the entire team stretch together before and after a game or practice. However, if your group does not warm up together, make sure you give yourself the necessary time to do it on your own. Note the key points described along with each stretch. In combination, they serve as a solid foundation for effective and pain-free stretching for hockey players.

Wrist Rolls

Start your stretching routine with the upper body, either in the neck/shoulder area or in the arms or wrists (figure 1.2). Never begin stretching in the lower body. Don't go into leg lunges or any form of groin stretch too soon.

Figure 1.2   Wrist rolls

Shoulder Rolls

Shoulder rolls are designed to loosen the trunk and shoulders. Look straight ahead and don't overextend the rotation (figure 1.3).

Shoulder Dips

Shoulder dips are excellent for working on the shoulders while loosening the trunk and hamstrings (figure 1.4). When

Figure 1.3 Shoulder rolls

Figure 1.4 Shoulder dips

possible, use a partner for shoulder girdle stretching in conjunction with the previous shoulder stretches.

Hatchet

The lower back can suffer tremendous strain due to the nature of hockey. Therefore, it is very imporant to stretch this region of the body (figure 1.5).

Figure 1.5   Hatchet

Seal Stretch

Stretch like a cat, slowly and fully extending. Hold the stretch for only 5 to 10 seconds (figure 1.6).

Figure 1.6   Seal stretch

Toe Touch

Always flex the knee slightly. Don't stand straight legged. No need to rip the capsule surrounding the knee (figure 1.7).

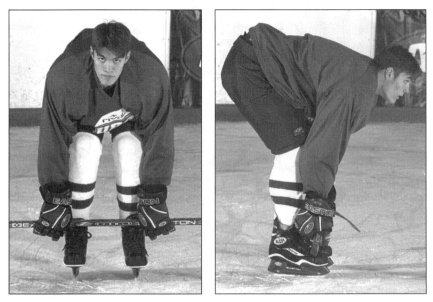

Figure 1.7   Toe touch

Lower-Body Load

Keep the head level with your eyes looking forward as you flex and stretch the muscles in the upper leg and groin areas (figure 1.8).

Figure 1.8   Lower-body load

Heel Press

Work up to this stretch as your flexibility improves. Remember to spread the legs slowly as the stick is placed between your heels (figure 1.9).

Figure 1.9   Heel press

Hamstring Heaven

Maximize the effect of this stretch throughout your back, leg, and groin areas by tucking your chin close to your chest (figure 1.10).

Figure 1.10   Hamstring heaven

Groin Stretch

A traditional hockey stretch which should be done at the end of your stretching routine. This will ensure that the big muscle groups of the leg and buttock areas are loose and filled with blood before stretching (figure 1.11).

Summary

We suggest that serious hockey players remember the four essentials described in this chapter.

1. Get the right skates for you.
2. Key on proper posture and balance points for proper skating.
3. Develop lower-body strength to improve technique.
4. Do a warm-up routine in advance of skill development.

Figure 1.11   Groin stretch

By following this advice hockey players and skaters from other disciplines will find that they can dramatically increase their ability to perform. We want you to achieve maximum performance with minimum effort. By following the advice in this chapter you will move closer to achieving that goal. In the next chapter we will begin to analyze skating by looking at forward skating, the basis for all skating technique to follow.

2

Forward Skating

As a beginning hockey player you have made the decision to learn how to skate properly. Or perhaps as a veteran player you realize that your skating must improve if you ever hope to get to the next level. Maybe you are currently asking yourself, "Now what?" Simply putting in more ice time won't help if all you manage to do is continue reinforcing bad habits. What you need is some kind of systematic skating road map to help you improve one step at a time toward your goal of becoming a better skater.

Take heart, because the road map is about to unfold before you.

Beginning with this chapter we will examine the various components of skating in a systematic way—one that has been tried, tested, and proven successful over time. Specifically, we are going to break down skating mechanics by describing key elements within each skill, emphasizing both lower- and upper-body components. Each section will use photos to give a visual representation of what we are describing. To provide you with the information you need to move along this skating road map, this and each succeeding chapter will be presented according to the following criteria:

1. A detailed description of key elements for each skill set.
2. Common problems associated with learning a skill and reference to drills in the chapter that will improve technique.
3. A series of drills to use for reinforcing the skill set.

The drills in this chapter, like those in the rest of the book, are useful to players at virtually any level. We generally present the drills from simple to increasingly difficult in a progressive format. They represent a selection of fun and challenging activities that will test even the best skaters on their abilities while working on technique. We have also included helpful tips and guidelines in the Key Points portion of each activity.

Although it might be tempting to skip ahead to some of the more advanced activities, players who seek to develop well-rounded skating technique must first master the basic drills. Even professional players spend time practicing the basics in their day-to-day workouts. With that in mind, let's turn our attention to the pursuit of improving your forward skating.

Forward skating is the fundamental building block for almost all skill development in hockey. The components of forward skating described and shown in this chapter affect the game through a wide range of game-related activities. For example, you prepare to skate into a corner of the rink, ready to battle for a loose puck. Unless you have sound edge control to maintain balance, the results could be disastrous. Or your opponent turns over the puck in the neutral zone, presenting you with a goal-scoring opportunity. Make sure your focus is on the task of scoring, with the head level and eyes on target (figure 2.1). Eventually, as your skating becomes second nature, you should not have to concentrate on skating technique during these game situations.

You must refine forward skating so that it is automatic. Only then can you develop the additional skills needed to play hockey at its highest levels. We are about to examine the three key elements of forward skating, then identify common problems associated with developing specific skills within each element. In addition, we will recommend an activity from the drill section of this chapter, which will assist in correcting the problem within each element.

Key Elements:

1. Stride

2. Glide

3. Recovery

Figure 2.1 Head level with the eyes on target

Stride, glide, and recovery are the basic components of forward skating. Stop for a moment and think about the skating motion of an accomplished player such as Mark Messier. As he skates forward, his upper- and lower-body regions are coordinated into a unique rhythm that he has developed over many years of practice. While his style of skating will be his alone, the basic components of stride, glide, and recovery are there for you just as they are for him. You might ask, "If the basics are the same for everyone, why can't I skate like Mark Messier?" You can find part of the reason in the problems associated with learning and refining these three key elements. We will first describe each skating element in detail, then explain some problem areas that you should consider as you practice forward skating.

Stride Leg or Stride Phase

The stride leg is the power source for each pushing motion during the striding phase of forward skating. This action originates in the hip area, goes through the knee, and finishes with full extension of the ankle. The stride leg when fully extended should be turned to approximately a 45-degree angle relative to the direction the skater is headed. The weight should be on the ball of the foot, primarily on the inside edge of the blade. When you execute a full extension properly, from a side view you should be able to draw an imaginary straight line from the ankle area of the boot, up through the knee and hip, finishing the line with your shoulders and head.

To the untrained participant or observer, forward skating might look like a skill that has all its mechanics centered in the lower body. But looks can be deceiving. At elite levels of play upper-body control will influence top-end speed, balance, and agility. Remember while striding that leaning too far forward may cause the stride skate to come off the ice before you reach a full stride. Also, much as players often substitute bending too far forward at the waist for knee bend, so too can wild arm movement be interpreted as furthering skating speed. It doesn't. Keep the arms under control while striding. Move them forward and backward, not side to side. During the forward-skating elements you should have just one hand on your stick when you do not have the puck. Put two hands on the stick only when you are about to receive a pass or as you prepare to stick handle or take a shot. Otherwise, for straightaway, breakaway speed it is better to have only one hand, your top hand, on the stick shaft.

Common Problems

• Try to keep your skate edges in contact with the ice as long as possible. This guarantees that you will have a surface to push off from, whereas skates that are off the ice have only air as a contact surface, and that is not easy to grip. Corrective drills are 1 and 5.

• Make sure that your ankles are not leaning inward or outward at extreme angles. If this continues to occur it may be the result of skates that do not provide proper support. Corrective drills are 1, 2, and 5.

• Newer players are often tentative when trying to master edge control. Remember that Bobby Orr, Wayne Gretzky, and the other greats spent time falling to learn good edge-control technique. Push yourself to see where your limits are in edge-control work. Corrective drills are 2, 5, and 6.

• The toe of your stride skate should not point straight down toward the ice at the completion of a stride. This will result in heel kick, causing a loss in both speed and balance. The corrective drill is 5.

• Focus on finishing each stride by pushing from the hip through the knee to the ankle. This will give you a longer, smoother stride rather than a shorter, choppier look that comes from a lack of extension. Corrective drills are 3 and 5.

• Your arms should be in a distinctive rhythm during your forward-skating stride, acting to assist your skating by moving forward and backward, not side to side, much like the arm action of a sprinter. Watch that the upper half of the arm, elbow to shoulder, does not cross over the midline of the body. The corrective drill is 4.

Glide Phase

This part of the skating motion is short in duration. As its name implies, the player is gliding rather than pushing, recovering with the opposite skate in this part of the forward-skating sequence. During the glide phase the skate blade of the support leg is on the flat of the blade with the weight over the ball of the foot (figure 2.2). In addition, the leg has close to a 90-degree bend during this phase. This aspect of the skating motion works as a launching pad with the leg positioned to exert as much force as possible through the next pushing motion.

This position is unique to skating, and newer players seldom use it. Many players have a problem holding this position because they lack leg strength in the key muscle group used in gliding, the quadriceps. With increased strength and proper instruction, poor posture can be corrected and the glide leg

Figure 2.2 The glide phase

can become an important and positive aspect of proper skating technique. As with the striding phase, your upper body must square the shoulders over the hips with the chest out and the head up. But remember that younger, inexperienced players may need to have their eyes down looking at the puck to maintain control. Be patient and work toward less head-down activity, which will result in the chest being more upright. Of course, this takes time and practice.

Common Problems

• Check that the skate of the support leg is not off the midline of the body. If it is, poor balance will result. The corrective drill is 3.

• Do not place your weight on the inside edge of the support-leg skate blade. Players who have weak ankles often do this. Corrective drills are 1 and 5.

• Ensure that your head is directly over your support leg. Your arms should not cross the midline of the body. Corrective drills are 3 and 5.

Recovery Phase

The recovery phase, the final key element in successful skating, refers to retrieving the push, or stride, leg back underneath the body. Once you have achieved full extension with the stride leg, you must raise the skate slightly off the ice surface and return the foot directly under the body. The skate should return in a straight line, meaning that the front of the skate is pointed exactly in the intended direction of flight while resting on the flats of the blade (figure 2.3). The stride leg then becomes the support leg before your next stride.

Figure 2.3   The recovery phase

Throughout all three phases of forward skating you must resist the urge to lower your head, which will cause you to look down. Some players use a stick that is too short, often resulting in the head looking down rather than out. Check stick length so that you aren't putting yourself at a disadvantage. Something this simple can have a dramatic impact on your skating style and efficiency during each skating phase.

Finally, you won't see world-class sprinters running down the track with their arms moving across their bodies opposite the direction they are headed. The arms move toward their target. As previously noted, hockey players should attempt to mirror this action. Try to ensure that your upper arm does not cross the midline of your upper body while forward skating. Players who move their arms across their bodies are often said to be "pitching hay" with their sticks. This will restrict each skating stride. The player will not fully benefit from the energy used in each stride because the stride skate will lose contact with the ice before the leg reaches full extension.

Common Problems

- As recovery occurs ensure that you get on the flats of the blade to maximize your glide. Staying too long on either the inside or outside edge is counterproductive. Corrective drills are 3 and 5.

- Watch for movements laterally, or side to side, because any action that causes the body to go sideways will always slow you down. We all learned in math class that the shortest distance between two points is a straight line. Players should attempt to follow a straight path as well, not a zigzag route, for maximum skating efficiency. Corrective drills are 3, 4, and 5.

Summary

To be an effective forward skater you must have both the upper- and lower-body regions working in combination to create a fluid skating style. It is important to have many skating activities that effectively isolate these two regions so that you can begin to *feel* proper technique. After you have practiced and mastered these techniques in isolation, you can combine movement in the two regions to produce an automatic set of skills, skills that are well conceived and trained to be technically correct and advantageous to your forward-skating mechanics and style.

Now that we have looked at the basics of forward skating, we can move on to other areas of interest. We will refer to many of the ideas described in this chapter as we continue to examine skating as the primary means of improving your hockey skills.

Drill Section Notes

The drills that accompany this section on forward skating are designed to give you basic-level activities, which will force you to focus on proper upper- and lower-body mechanics. We present the six drills in a natural progression and recommend that you do them in order (1 to 6). Try to feel the different edges of your blades while attempting a drill, and remember to include sound posture in the upper body as well. These drills are not designed for high speed initially; instead you should be concentrating on perfect technique and mechanics. Once your technique improves, you can increase speeds. You should be focusing on body awareness, control, and technique above all else.

① ONE-LEGGED GLIDE

Purpose

To practice edge control, balance, and proper gliding technique using only one leg. To develop proper positioning between the upper and lower body.

Procedure

1. Begin by standing at one end of the rink, take three or four strides, and then glide on only one skate blade.
2. Tuck your nonglide leg behind the glide leg so that only one skate remains on the ice.
3. By distributing your weight over the ball of the foot with the skate straight up and down, you should be able to achieve equal pressure on both blade edges.
4. You should concentrate on maintaining proper posture with your chin in a straight line with the knee and toes of your glide leg.

Key Points

• This drill is designed to make you aware of proper alignment, so focus on 90-degree knee bend as a way of achieving good balance.

• Do not allow your weight to move too far forward to the toes or too far back toward your heels. Rather, attempt to distribute your weight evenly over the ball of the foot to maximize your glide, balance, and control.

• Do not allow your eyes to track downward, something that skaters who lack confidence will do. Keep the head still and the eyes focused on an imaginary target in the distance.

ONE-LEGGED GLIDE **1**

2 LEG LOADING

Purpose

To introduce efficient knee bend while practicing edge and balance control. To establish a proper pushing action from the hip, through the knee, and to the ankle (extension).

Procedure

1. Begin at one end of the rink by bending the right leg close to 90 degrees at the knee joint.
2. Apply pressure to the inside edge of the skate blade of the left leg and push off, shifting body weight on to your other leg as you leap laterally (photo a).
3. As your weight moves to the right leg, load up the right knee joint by bending to 90 degrees, apply pressure on the inside edge of that skate, and again push off. Your weight should move back to your left side (photo b).
4. Continue this action the length of the rink, alternating leg loads as you move down the ice.

Key Points

• This will appear as a hopping or leaping action. But remember that you should not be jumping high in this drill; instead move laterally or side to side.

• Concentrate on your knee loading, getting close to 90 degrees each time, which will assist in extension.

• Your head and shoulders should remain level. Keep your arms under control, and if practicing with a stick, keep it in front rather than to the side of your body.

(a)

(b)

29

③ THREE-COUNT RECOVERY

Purpose

To reinforce proper balance and body alignment during the stride and glide phases of forward skating.

Procedure

1. Begin at one end of the rink with your stick held horizontally with both hands in front of you at shoulder height.
2. Take a stride forward with either leg, hold the glide position on the other leg, and count 1, 2, 3 to yourself (photo a). Then recover the stride-pushing leg under your body (photo b).
3. Focus on maintaining correct posture during the glide with the upper body still and the glide leg bent close to 90 degrees.

Key Points

• It is essential that the support, or glide, leg stay bent at 90 degrees with the toes of the skate on the flat of the blade. This will ensure that you do not drift side to side; rather you will skate or glide in a straight line.

• Try to finish each push by snapping the ankle for additional extension and push.

• Do not hurry this activity. Focus on proper recovery after you take each stride under the midline of the upper body.

THREE-COUNT RECOVERY 3

(a)

(b)

RAILROAD

Purpose

To introduce proper leg and arm rhythm while forward skating.

Procedure

1. Line up along the goal line at one end of the rink.
2. Begin moving forward by keeping your knees bent slightly and the toes pointing straight ahead while sliding your skates forward and backward (photo a).
3. At the same time, concentrate on moving your left arm forward as you push backward with the left leg, followed by your right arm moving forward as you push back with your right leg (photo b). Continue this motion until you reach the far end of the rink.

Key Points

• Your skates should never leave the ice. They must slide forward and backward in a straight line as if attached to rails.

• You will discover that it is difficult to generate any speed if you cannot bend at the knee joint.

• This drill permits you to see that forward momentum can be positively affected by proper arm action.

• Be sure to keep the arms moving forward and backward only, not side to side.

RAILROAD 4

(a)

(b)

5 SCULLING

Purpose

To practice pushing off with the inside edge of either skate blade. To reinforce proper recovery of the skate under the body. To keep the support leg close to 90 degrees.

Procedure

1. Begin at one end of the rink and push by making a C-cut with either skate from the heel of the inside edge of the blade to start movement forward.
2. As you begin to slow down, recover the push or sculling leg under the body, then repeat the action with the same leg until you reach the end of the rink (photo a).
3. The opposite leg should remain under the midline with 90-degree knee bend and on the flat of the blade (photo b).
4. Return to where you started the drill by using the other leg in a similar fashion. You can try the drill again by combining first a left-foot scull, then a right-foot scull, alternating as you move along the ice.

Key Points

• Do not allow yourself to move too quickly. Rather, get as big of a bang as you can out of each pushing action by maximizing your extension from the hip through the knee and ankle joints.

• The head and shoulders should remain over the glide leg throughout this drill, with some arm movement to assist your forward motion.

• Focus on a deep knee bend and maintain it throughout.

• Push from the heel of the stride skate using the inside of the blade to make a C-cut.

• The skate recovers under the midline without losing contact with the ice.

(a)

(b)

6 FROG LEAPS

Purpose

To develop leg strength while mastering control of the inside edges of both skate blades.

Procedure

1. Begin at one end of the rink with your skates placed in a V formation in which you point your heels toward each other (photo a).
2. Allow your body weight to move toward the heels of your skates. Push using the inside edges away from the midline of the body (photo b). When the skates are beyond shoulder-width apart, leap forward, focusing on going out, not just up. Pull the skates back underneath you while in the air (photo c).
3. Recover both legs under the body and repeat this motion until you reach the opposite end of the rink.

Key Points

• You will look like a frog leaping down the ice, hence the name of the activity.

• Try to recover both feet directly under your body by touching the skates together to ensure proper recovery.

• Keep your head up, your shoulders over your hips, and your eyes looking at a target at the other end of the ice surface.

• Picture yourself as a long jumper while doing this activity. Like a long jumper, your goal is to get as much distance forward as possible. Don't jump in the air too high because this will reduce forward distance.

(a)

(b)

(c)

3

Backward Skating

You suddenly find yourself playing against four attacking opponents who are whirling out of the neutral zone into your end of the rink. In an instant you pivot, change to backward skating, and temporarily hold off the onslaught at your defensive blue line. Or perhaps you become a member of the power-play unit and are forced to "walk the line" as you attempt to create time and space for your teammates. You maneuver backward along the blue line, setting up the winning goal as time runs out.

In these game situations proficient backward skating is a necessity, not a luxury. Being able to move into efficient backward skating can prove beneficial whether you are the attacker or find yourself being attacked. Backward skating isn't just for defenders anymore.

Once a player has established the proper mechanics for forward skating, the next step is to turn around and learn to skate backward. This is easier said than done. At every level of hockey, including the National Hockey League, many players have difficulty mastering backward mobility. In this section we will follow the format of the previous chapter by breaking down this skill into key stages, all of which we included in our forward-skating analysis. With some simple adjustments in technique most players can become proficient backward skaters, often capable of skating as fast backward as forward. We'll begin this chapter by examining the key elements of backward skating.

Key Elements:

1. C-cuts
2. Crossover method

In backward skating you must learn the basic elements of C-cuts and crossovers if you wish to develop successful skating technique. We will use the term *crossover* often in this book because it is an important element in many types of skating maneuvers. Both C-cuts and crossovers are critical to generating speed in backward skating. You should become competent at both because game situations may require you to execute either move. Although the two skills are centered in the movements of the legs and lower body, posture is important for each. The positioning of the upper body varies from what you read in the previous chapter on forward skating. We will detail each skill by describing the lower- and upper-body characteristics.

C-Cuts

As in forward skating, the C-cut has stride, recovery, and glide components that must be isolated and mastered if the skater is to execute the skill properly. For a proper C-cut, the support leg should be bent close to 90 degrees and positioned directly under the body in a direct line with the chin (figure 3.1). Players should distribute weight over the ball of the foot with the flat of the blade in contact with the ice. Many players do not achieve enough bend in this leg and thus cannot achieve maximum power. The skater must concentrate on keeping both the knee and ankle bent, ensuring that posture is not too straight.

While the support leg acts to balance you during a C-cut, the stride leg plays a critical role in generating skating speed. This leg action should begin in front of the support skate, not beside it (figure 3.2).

The key in achieving success is to cut the letter C into the ice with the stride skate, having your skate follow a semicircular cutting motion ahead of the support, or glide, skate. Unlike

Figure 3.1 Correct C-cut posture

Figure 3.2 C-cut leg action

weight distribution on the support leg, the weight for all stride-leg maneuvers should be placed over the ball of your foot while resting primarily on the inside edge of the blade (figure 3.3). You should push from the hip area, extending through the knee and ankle joints to finish the stroke.

The recovery phase occurs immediately after you complete the C-cut (figure 3.4). You pick up the stride leg and bring it back under the body in a straight line to its original support position. The skate blade should not drag along the ice surface during recovery; rather it should remain in contact with the ice. Once you complete the recovery phase, the stride leg becomes the support leg before the next striding motion.

The glide phase in a C-cut is the time when a player has completed the C-cut motion and is bringing that skate back

Figure 3.3 C-cut finish

Figure 3.4 C-cut recovery, preparing for the next stride

under the midline of the body. From a front view we should be able to see a straight-line relationship between the chin, knee, and toe (figure 3.5). Efficient posture is important in backward skating, with the upper-body regions being somewhat straighter or more upright compared with forward skating. Everything starts at the top. If you do not position the head properly the upper body can adversely affect all the lower-body actions. We know that you generate most of your power and speed through the proper execution of lower-body mechanics. But as in forward skating, the upper body plays a significant role in achieving maximum efficiency in backward skating. Refer to the list of upper-body considerations provided just before the drills section of this chapter for important key points.

Figure 3.5   Front view of the C-cut

Common Problems

• Check knee bend for maximum power. Many skaters fail to maintain a sitting position with the knees bent and back relatively straight. This can result in the upper torso leaning too far forward which affects balance while attempting a C-cut. Corrective drills are 7 and 8.

• Too much heel weighting will cause poor balance and often result in a tumble to the ice. This occurs because the outside edge of the blade will bite into the ice rather than continuing to glide. Remember that the weight should not be on the heels; instead distribute it over the ball of the foot on both skates. Corrective drills are 7, 8, and 12.

• Focus on achieving extension at the knee and the ankle for maximum power and efficiency during the stride phase. Players who fail to do this look choppy and cannot reach their full speed potential during drills. Corrective drills are 10 and 11.

• Many younger players will wiggle their bottoms, which indicates that they have not transferred weight from one skate to the other. Pivoting becomes a difficult skill to master from this position. Corrective drills are 9 and 10.

• Often players will start the stride phase of the technique to the side of the support leg rather than slightly in front. This leads to a side-to-side motion rather than straight-line movement down the ice. A player must complete the C-cut ahead of the support, or glide, skate. Corrective drills are 9 and 10.

• Players who do not use their inside edge during a C-cut will find that their skates will slide on the flats of the blade, resulting in no power or speed. The corrective drill is 10.

• Do not allow "lazy skates," in which the skater drags the blade along the ice. This will slow recovery time and impede overall speed. The corrective drill is 9.

• Players often do not completely return the recovery leg under the midline of the body. This results in poor balance, which affects a skater's ability to pivot or generate maximum speed and power. The corrective drill is 9.

• Do not turn skates inward during the glide phase, using the inside edges rather than the flats of the blades. This usually results when a player fails to recover under the midline of the upper body. Corrective drills are 7 and 9.

• Excessive arm swinging or restricted arm movements will negatively affect C-cuts. Work to develop the proper rhythm in arm movements between the stride, glide, and recovery. The left arm goes forward as the left skate makes the C-cut and recovers to your side as the skate recovers under the body midline. The corrective drill is 9.

Crossover Method

This type of backward skating shares many characteristics of the C-cut method with some important exceptions. First, you generate speed in crossovers by picking up one leg and crossing it in front of the other as you apply force backward after the C-cut has been made (figure 3.6). This requires that you develop good balance because your weight will move onto the outside edge of the leg being crossed. In addition, try to limit your crossover action to only one step in each direction. This will keep you moving backward rather than side to side.

The key differences in movement compared with the C-cut is evident in the push from the leg that passes behind or underneath the crossover leg. The sequence for the skater is

Figure 3.6   The crossover move

to make the C-cut motion as noted in the previous section. In this technique, however, the striding skate crosses in front of the support, or glide, skate. As the skates cross, the player transfers upper-body weight to the skate that just completed the C-cut. This allows the skater to push off the outside edge of the underneath skate. The skater then lifts the underneath skate off the ice, pulling it back underneath the midline of the upper body. To execute this crossover method effectively, skaters must concentrate on the three aspects of the technique— C-cut, crossunder, and step through. During the crossover method the upper body tracks the stepping skate and you shift weight from one side to the other as the legs cross. If you do not have good control of your outside edges, it will be difficult to master the crossover move. Center the weight over the balls of the feet on both skates.

Note that crossover is a misleading term in that the crossing skate is not actually being picked off the ice and moved over top of the support, or glide, skate. Rather, the crossing skate is pulled across in front of the other skate.

Common Problems

• Watch for the upper body leaning too far forward at the waist. This causes balance problems for the lower body, especially in the support leg, and restricts the stride motion as well. The corrective drill is 9.

• Players will often bring their arms across the body midline, forcing a side-to-side drifting rather than a straight-line motion backward. The corrective drill is 9.

• Often players will cross over only to the midbody line, which is not a real crossover at all. As a result, speed is generated from only one skate. The corrective drill is 11.

Whether attempting a C-cut or crossover it is important that you focus on maintaining upper-body position in conjunction with lower-body technique. Remember these important upper-body considerations.

1. Keep your head level and eyes looking forward, not down.

2. Have your shoulders always parallel to the ice and square to the direction of travel.

3. Your back should be straight with a slight lean forward at the waist. Note, however, that you should not position your head out over the toes as a result of this forward lean.

4. Your support leg may not be at 90 degrees. Many young players don't possess the leg strength necessary to hold this position.

5. Arm movement is similar to forward skating, only not as exaggerated.

6. Carry your stick with the top hand only, with the palm of the hand facing the ice.

Once you learn to use both C-cuts and crossovers effectively, you will find backward skating easier to master. Practice these key elements so that you become proficient at both because game situations may require you to execute either move.

Summary

Backward skating has often been dismissed as a skill that only defenders need to master. The modern game of hockey, however, requires that *all* players be able to move with precision and ease from forward to backward skating. By first reinforcing the proper mechanics discussed in this chapter, the stage is set for an easy introduction to puck control while in the backward position. Without these essential mechanics you will find backward skating, backward pivoting, turning, and puck control difficult and frustrating.

We have now described the basic components of both forward and backward skating. The next part of this book will detail a skill that all players must be able to execute properly to play hockey at its highest levels. Let's examine our *starting.*

Drill Section Notes

The six drills included in this chapter will allow you to isolate all the important skill components of backward skating. These activities force you to practice and refine the various leg and ankle movements required for both C-cut and crossover strategies. These drills will also provide you the opportunity to monitor and correct your upper-body positioning as discussed in this chapter.

As you attempt a drill remember that it is not a race to see who can finish first. Only after you have achieved proper mechanics should you attempt to move at faster speeds. If you do not have experience with backward skating, be prepared for some fatigue as you work through the activities. Keeping proper knee bend while skating backward taxes the leg muscles.

ONE-LEGGED BACK GLIDE

Purpose

To practice backward edge control, balance, and proper gliding technique using one leg only. To develop proper positioning between the upper and lower body.

Procedure

1. This drill is similar to forward-skating drill 1. Begin by standing at one end of the rink prepared to skate backward. Take three or four strides and then glide on one skate blade only.
2. Tuck your nonglide leg behind the glide leg so that only one skate remains on the ice.
3. By distributing your weight along the glide blade you should be able to achieve equal pressure on the blade edges. Center your weight over the ball of the foot.
4. Concentrate on maintaining proper posture with your chin in a straight line with the knee and toes of your glide leg.

Key Points

• This drill is designed to make you aware of proper alignment, so focus on sound knee bend as a way of achieving good balance.

• Do not allow your weight to move too far forward to the toes of your feet or too far back toward your heels. Rather, attempt to keep equal pressure on both the inside and outside edges of the glide skate. If you can glide in a straight line you have achieved equal pressure.

• Do not allow your eyes to track downward, something that many skaters do when they are unsure of themselves. Keep the head still and the eyes focused on a distant target.

ONE-LEGGED BACK GLIDE

8 BACKWARD LEG LOAD

Purpose

To introduce efficient knee bend while practicing edge and balance control. To establish a proper backward pushing action from the hip, through the knee, and to the ankle using full extension. To develop leg strength.

Procedure

1. This drill is similar to forward drill 2. Begin at one end of the rink by bending the right leg close to 90 degrees at the knee joint as you prepare to skate backward (photo a).
2. Apply pressure to the inside edge of the skate blade of the right leg and push off with a C-cut, shifting body weight to your other leg as you leap laterally (photo b).
3. As your weight moves to the left leg, load up the left knee joint, apply pressure on the inside edge of that skate, and again push and extend from the hip (photo c). Your weight should move back to your right side.
4. Continue this action the length of the rink, alternating leg loads as you move down the ice.

Key Points

• This will appear as a hopping or leaping action. Remember that you should not be attempting to jump high in this drill. Rather, leap laterally or side to side.

• Concentrate on your knee loading, getting close to 90 degrees each time to assist in extension.

• Your head and shoulders should remain level. Keep your arms under control. If practicing with a stick keep it in front of your body rather than to the side.

• Keep your weight over the balls of the feet.

(a)

(b)

(c)

⑨ C-CUT RECOVERY

Purpose

To reinforce proper balance and body alignment during the stride and glide phases of backward skating.

Procedure

1. This drill is similar to drill 3 in forward skating. Begin at one end of the rink with your stick held horizontally with both hands in front of you at shoulder height as you prepare to skate backward.
2. Make a C-cut with either leg, glide on the opposite leg and count 1, 2, 3 to yourself, then recover the push leg under your body.
3. Focus on maintaining correct posture during the glide with the upper body still and the glide, or support, leg bent close to 90 degrees.

Key Points

- It is essential that the support, or glide, leg stay bent with the toes of the skate pointed directly forward. This will ensure that you do not drift side to side; rather you will move backward in a straight line.
- Try to finish each stride by snapping the ankle for additional power and push during the C-cut.
- Do not hurry this activity. Focus on proper glide and recovery after you take each stride.

C-CUT RECOVERY

⑩ ALTERNATE C-CUTS

Purpose

To reinforce proper C-cut technique for both legs.

Procedure

1. Begin at one end of the rink by using a sound C-cut push to get you in motion backward (photo a). You must complete the C-cut ahead of the support, or glide, skate.
2. As you recover the initial push leg under the body midline, touch your ankles together, then begin another C-cut motion with your other leg (photo b).
3. Continue to follow this alternating pattern as you skate the length of the ice, making sure to take a moment between each stride to set up for a perfect C-cut every time.

Key Points

• You must keep the support leg close to 90 degrees in preparation for the next C-cut that will occur.

• Your upper body should remain still in the proper position, in which the head is up and the eyes are looking out, not at the ice. Bend your elbows, with the stick positioned directly in front of your body, not to the side.

• Remember to pause briefly between each alternate push as a means of preparing for excellent technique.

(a)

(b)

11 C-CUT, CROSSOVER STEP THROUGH

Purpose

To refine both the C-cut and crossover backward-skating techniques by using a single drill. To practice edge control and proper weight distribution and balance.

Procedure

1. Begin at one end of the ice with your legs shoulder-width apart and knees bent to 90 degrees (photo a). Initiate a powerful C-cut with the leg of your choice (photo b).
2. Once you complete the C-cut maintain pressure to the inside edge of the same skate blade and make an additional cross in front of the support leg (photo c).
3. Complete the move by putting pressure on the outside edge of the initial support leg, then push off the outside edge and pull it back underneath so that your two skates are now in the ready position, shoulder-width apart.

Key Points

• Do this drill slowly, focusing on proper weight distribution and edge control.

• Keep the upper body tracking the lower body as the shift in balance occurs. If practicing with a stick do not allow it to drag behind your body; always keep it in front.

• Center your weight over the balls of the feet in both skates.

(a)

(b)

(c)

HOURGLASS

Purpose

To practice pushing off with the inside edge of both skate blades while backward skating. To develop balance on skate edges.

Procedure

1. Start at one end of the rink facing backward with skates in the ready position, remembering to keep the knees bent.
2. Turn the front toe area of each skate inward toward each other, allowing your weight to be over the balls of the feet (photo a). Push on both skates at the same time, which will cause the legs to begin spreading apart (photo b).
3. Once the skates are outside the shoulder line, turn the heels toward each other and recover both skates under your body. Attempt to touch both ankles together during this recovery stage.
4. Continue to replicate this figure-8 formation repeatedly with your skates, which will produce an hourglass shape over a distance.

Key Points

• Your weight should be primarily on the inside edges of both skate blades with strong knee bend for maximum efficiency.

• Do not allow your upper body to fall too far forward at the waist because this will negatively impact knee bend and balance.

• Begin by making a fairly tight or skinny hourglass shape, then grow the pattern wider as your balance improves and your confidence in your edge control increases.

(a)

(b)

4

Starting

At some point in every hockey game you will find yourself in a stationary position. You are about to execute another skating start. This may occur during a face-off encounter, while standing in front of an opponent's goaltender for screening purposes, or even after being hit to the ice by a thunderous check. In all three situations, you must be able to move quickly from a static starting position to rejoin the action immediately.

At times such as these you don't have to be the fastest skater to win the race. For example, Erik Lindros isn't always the fastest straight-ahead skater on the ice, yet he is able to compete for loose pucks off a static start because of his foot speed and quickness from a dead stop. If you can develop quickness through starting technique, you can reduce the overall time you require to reach maximum speed.

In this chapter we will describe the two most common start positions and detail how to improve your overall skating quickness and speed by improving your start. Note as well the special section at the end of this chapter that describes and illustrates a unique method for assessing proper starting action. This simple assessment tool, known at Huron as *skate-print analysis,* can provide players with invaluable information regarding their starting motion. We recommend that players and coaches alike learn this technique as a sure way of improving hockey starts.

Key Elements:

1. V start
2. Crossover start

You might have previously attended a hockey school or read information about various types of skating starts that have unique names. We use the terms *V start* and *crossover start* because these seem to be generally accepted across a wide range of hockey instructors, experts, and coaches. As we describe these starts you might identify them by another name, and that's fine. We have chosen specific titles for these two key elements of starting to help standardize some of the language associated with skating. Regardless of the terminology, by improving your starting technique you have the opportunity to improve your total skating speed, which you must develop if you intend to move up the hockey ladder. Let's begin by looking at the V start.

V Start

This type of starting action gained its name from the positioning of the skates as the starting action is initiated. The heels of both skates touching and the toes flared out in opposite directions form the letter V, hence the name (figure 4.1). It is important that you focus on keeping the knees bent as you initiate this start. Concentrate on developing three quick, explosive steps without a glide as you begin this action rather than starting with a striding action. Center your weight on the balls of the feet and on your inside skate edges.

What you want to do with any start is initiate momentum. With this objective a stride motion is not the quickest way to begin. You must also understand that with a V start you are attempting to move *forward*, not *upward*. Using the long-jump analogy again, the ideal V start would see your knees bent throughout, with your head and shoulders level as you begin the three-step sequence. Don't look down off the start. The ice isn't going anywhere, it's not going to melt, so focus on a target in front of you. This will help you keep your knees bent and your upper body in a good mechanical position.

Figure 4.1 The V start

After you have taken the first three steps your body should begin to rise slightly from the power position of knees bent, and your standard forward-skating technique described in chapter 2 will take over. Try to keep your back relatively straight and point your chest toward your intended direction of travel. Keep your arms moving in a straight line forward and backward as described in the forward-skating section, with the stick in one hand pointed in the direction you want to go. Don't let that stick drag off to the side of your body because that will decrease overall quickness. As you step forward toward your intended direction of travel, you must push off the inside edge of either skate blade and land on the inside edge of the other blade. You must rotate the toe of the stepping skate 90 degrees to your direction of travel to eliminate any glide action in the first three steps.

Common Problems

• Watch that your eyes stay focused on a point in the distance given the direction of the start. Too often players will look down, causing the legs to straighten, which means less power as you initiate the V start. Also, do not allow the upper body to lean too far forward. Lead with the chest, not the head. The corrective drill is 15.

• Some players will use a long stride to begin the starting sequence. Try to avoid any gliding during the first three steps because this will reduce your quickness off the start. The corrective drill is 14.

• Do not get too far up on your toes. Doing so will result in poor balance, possibly causing you to fall forward to the ice. Keep your weight centered on the balls of the foot. The corrective drill is 13.

• Do not have two hands on your stick during a starting sequence because this will slow the start. This occurs because stick location may hinder your ability to keep your shoulders square, directly over your hips. Corrective drills are 14 and 15.

• Some players will swing their arms side to side rather than front to back, resulting in decreased quickness off the start. Corrective drills are 14 and 15.

Crossover Start

The crossover start is so designated because one leg is picked up and crossed over the other to initiate movement forward. When properly executed, the crossover requires a player to use only a single crossing action followed by an opening of the hip, resulting in a V-start look and feel. You can use this kind of start when you need to effect a change in direction off a start as you attempt to get back into play from a static position.

As you do in the V start, bend your knees close to 90 degrees to get explosion from your initial steps. Initiate the crossover start by rotating the upper body toward your intended direction of travel. This will make it possible to focus on having the stepping skate close to the ice surface while allowing you to finish on the blade's inside edge with the toe at approximately 90 degrees to your intended direction (figure 4.2). As you begin to shift your body weight at the initiation of the crossover, the majority of pressure will fall on the outside edge of your support leg.

To develop a quick crossover start you must push off this outside edge and pull that skate forward. Finish again on the inside edge with the toe at 90 degrees to your intended line of travel. Once the crossing leg hits the ice you will find that your body is setting up in another V-start formation. Ideally you should use only one crossing step. Follow this single step by using the inside skate to take a small step to bring you back into a V-start position. Using the inside edges, take two or three additional small steps to complete the start. Continue as previously described in the V-start technique, and you will be comfortably into a forward-skating sequence in the blink of an eye.

As always, your head and eyes should be up and looking in the intended direction of travel with your back relatively straight. Shoulders should remain square over the hips as well. By pointing your stick in the direction of travel you will dramatically improve your ability to have the lower body in proper position for moving toward your intended target area. Again, keep only one hand on the stick.

(a)

(b)

Figure 4.2 The crossover start

Common Problems

- Many players will take more than one crossing step, which is not ideal. This usually occurs because they initially fail to rotate the upper body toward the intended direction of travel. The corrective drill is 16.

- You might have a tendency to straighten your legs and stand up rather than keep your center of gravity low to the ice. Focus on moving laterally, not upward. The corrective drill is 17.

- Avoid taking long strides and gliding between any of the first three steps in the start sequence. Corrective drills are 16 and 17.

- Watch for a hopping action that may indicate that the crossing skate is going too high over, rather than around, the support-leg skate. Corrective drills are 16 and 17.

- Be aware of the lazy-stick syndrome in which you drag the stick behind the body instead of using it to lead into the direction of travel of the start. Corrective drills are 16 and 17.

- Watch that your shoulders don't dip side to side rather than staying level (horizontal) during the crossover start. The corrective drill is 13.

Skate-Print Analysis for Effective Starts

One of the most effective ways to reinforce proper starting technique visually is by using ice marks, what we refer to as skate prints, during a practice session. This is a teaching mechanism that requires all players to learn and identify the look of a proper starting sequence on the ice surface. Players achieve this through reciprocal teaching, that is, by having each player work with a partner or coach to determine start efficiency. We recommend that coaches get to the ice immediately after it has been resurfaced and set aside one portion with cones or pylons to keep players away from a designated area. This will guarantee clean or new ice for the drill, which in turn allows easier identification of prints. Now, how do you read skate prints?

First, understand that in both types of starts the initial three steps are vitally important. An effective start will have short, compressed lines that should look something like what is shown in figure 4.1a. On ice you might choose to highlight the skate prints with a magic marker, which will allow players to see their skating patterns more easily. Notice the first three marks on the new ice consist of short, deep cuts with the feet turned at approximately 90-degree angles to the intended line of travel for steps one, two, and three. After the fourth step you will note a glide mark beginning to form (figure 4.3). Thereafter, a striding phase takes effect, and the player is no longer starting.

The skate prints assessed in figure 4.4 are not so successful. Notice the length of the initial mark for step one. It is much too

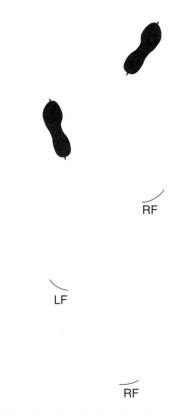

Figure 4.3 Successful skate prints for the V start

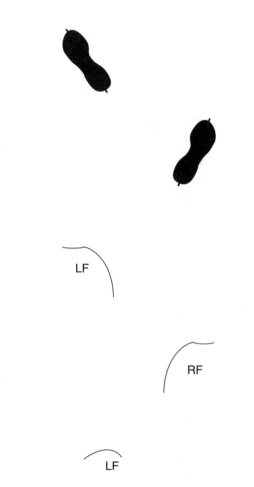

Figure 4.4 Unsuccessful skate prints for the V start

long, meaning that the skater didn't shift enough weight forward and didn't rotate the skate close to 90 degrees. Players will quickly come to understand the principles behind this drill and will enjoy doing it occasionally in practice. Coaches might consider including a monthly skate-print session so that players can see if they are making any progress in this facet of play.

It has been said that one picture is worth a thousand words. If you agree even in part with this statement, you'll undoubtedly see the benefits of using skate-print analysis as a visual means of reinforcing proper starting technique.

Summary

Hockey players should remember that during the start phase of skating the objective is to move forward, not upward. Many times we see players direct all their energy in the wrong direction. They stand up and lose knee bend in either a V or crossover start. One way to see this for yourself is to watch a starting sequence on video. Often you will notice the shoulders and head breaking the plane of the top of the arena boards, which form a horizontal line. Ideally, players will stay low in the start phase, keeping their shoulders parallel to the ice and on the same plane through the critical first three steps, and eventually rising slightly as they reach top speed.

By working with the skate-print technique players can learn which parts of their bodies are not technically in sync. They can then make appropriate adjustments. Once you understand how to explode off the start and quickly achieve maximum speed, you will need to learn how to stop. It is this difficult skill to which we will turn our attention in the next chapter.

Drill Section Notes

The selection of starting drills will touch on all the key components of starting. Some of the activities force you to slow down and walk through the start. This will give you the opportunity to visualize in slow motion how a proper starting technique should look and feel, from lower-body foot and knee position to head and shoulder components, as well as total upper-body lean. As in previous drill sections, we recommend that you walk before you skate. This means that you should be confident in the individual skills that make up a V or crossover start before going full speed.

In addition, when using a partner challenge him or her to give useful comments from the drills included in this section. Finally, come back to this section and try these drills as your hockey year progresses. Look at your starting skate prints in September and perhaps revisit this activity at midseason and near the end of the year. You should be able to see progress and deficiencies all by yourself, which will help you improve your starting technique in a self-corrective way.

13 DUCK WALK

Purpose

To teach proper skate and edge position as a lead-up activity to the V start.

Procedure

1. Players start from a stationary V-start position with skates turned in a V position and weight leaning on the inside edge of each skate and over the ball of each foot.
2. Skaters attempt to walk forward, stepping from inside edge to inside edge with the skate close to 90 degrees away from the direction of travel (photo a).
3. During this activity players should never pick up any skating momentum. Rather, they must walk over a designated distance while balancing on the inside skate edges (photo b).

Key Points

• It is essential to place your weight over the balls of the feet. Leaning too far forward or backward will result in a loss of balance.

• Use only the inside edges throughout this activity.

• Significant knee bend is a must in this drill.

• Keep your chest puffed out and leading the rest of your body.

• If your skates begin to glide it is usually a result of poor knee bend or because your weight is too far toward the heels rather than being on the balls of your feet.

DUCK WALK

(a)

(b)

14 THREE-STICK DRILL

Purpose

To practice proper V-start technique in an enjoyable activity while focusing on the first two steps of the start sequence.

Procedure

1. Place three sticks along the ice with approximately two to three feet separating each stick (photo a). Consider age and/or size of players, making the space between sticks larger or smaller depending on needs.
2. Players should stand in front of the first stick in a V-start position with their heels touching the stick shaft.
3. Players then execute a V start, moving between the remaining sticks, making sure not to touch any stick on their way through (photos b and c).
4. Players can work in pairs and take turns practicing the start while the partner observes and offers feedback.

Key Points

- If you glide too soon in either of your first two steps you will knock one of the two sticks. Focus on maintaining a 90-degree rotation on the stepping skate.
- If your weight is too far forward the push skate will slip backward and knock against the first stick. This often occurs if you begin the start with your head down and your eyes focused on the ice. Don't bend your waist excessively either.
- Focus on keeping the chest out to maintain proper balance, which will help generate speed.
- As you take a step, concentrate on landing on an inside edge, then drive hard by extending the push leg through to the knee and ankle without gliding.

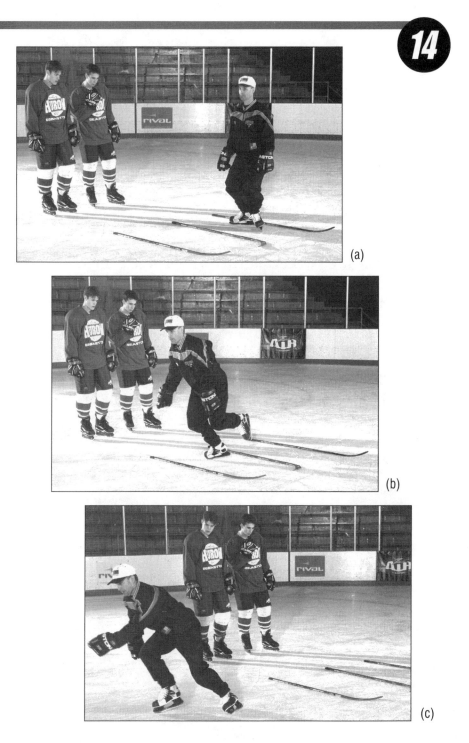

(a)

(b)

(c)

FALLING STICK

Purpose

To introduce the V start through a fun activity with a partner.

Procedure

1. Partners position themselves approximately six feet apart and hold their sticks upright with the toe of the blade in the air and the butt of the stick on the ice surface (photo a).
2. A coach or either partner initiates activity by saying "Ready." Both players assume a V-start position.
3. On the command "Go," players release their sticks and use a V start while attempting to move forward and catch their partner's stick before it falls to the ice (photos b and c).

Key Points

• Note that both players should begin with sticks in their right hands to create a skating lane. This will prevent crashes between partners. After a few attempts, both players switch to their left hands.

• Your eyes should be focused on the target, your partner's stick, rather than at your skates.

• Increase the distance between partners as players achieve success.

(a)

(b)

(c)

SIDEWAYS WALK

Purpose

As a lead-up drill to reinforce the crossover start.

Procedure

1. Begin by having players along any of the lines in the neutral-zone area.
2. All players must stand sideways to the intended direction of travel (photo a).
3. With the stick at shoulder level and arms extended in front of the body, the player brings the crossing skate in front of the support leg and lands on the inside edge (photo b).
4. The player then brings the support leg back through by taking ice laterally along the line to complete the move. The player continues the distance of the line to complete the drill.

Key Points

• Your head must follow your stepping skate to ensure proper balance.

• Keep your shoulders consistently parallel to the ice, not dipping side to side.

• Excessive straightening at the knees will result in your stick and head moving up and down rather than remaining in a constant position.

• Direct your momentum laterally, not vertically.

• Attempt the drill in both directions.

SIDEWAYS WALK

(a)

(b)

17 COACH'S COMMAND

Purpose

To practice proper execution of each phase of the crossover start.

Procedure

1. This is a followup to drill 16, with the emphasis on waiting for a coach's command to move (photo a).
2. As players execute each phase, coaches offer specific feedback on that aspect of the crossover start (photo b).
3. The coach will follow a similar sequence, calling for players to "Look, step, step through, and go" as each phase unfolds (photo c).

Key Points

• You must initiate the start by looking toward the intended direction of travel, making sure to point your stick in that direction as well.

• Then you must rotate your shoulders in the same direction.

• Try to focus on keeping your upper body tracking the stepping skate, keeping proper balance as you move.

• As the inside skate steps through, rotate the toe close to 90 degrees with your weight over the ball of your skate.

(a)

(b)

(c)

5

Stopping

Possessing the skill to stop on a dime is a prerequisite for any hockey player. In an instant you may be called upon to convert from offensive to defensive positioning. This skill will often depend on your ability to execute instantaneously some form of stopping action. Penalty killing is a classic application of this skill. Most coaches encourage this special-teams unit to incorporate stop-and-go patterns of skating rather than making big turns, which take too much time and can be costly while defending.

On a more pragmatic note, imagine yourself about to be run over by a huge, fire-breathing opponent who has you lined up for a big hit. In this situation it would surely be helpful to be able to stop quickly and sidestep the attacker. Even in hockey, intelligence, not courage, is sometimes the greater part of valor. Being in control of stopping skills will let you live to skate another day.

Just as you have learned how to effect proper starting technique in chapter 4, you will learn here the fundamentals of efficient stopping mechanics. In this chapter we will show you how to use two stops to your skating advantage. Many times during a game, stopping will be a key in determining which team controls the puck, especially following a turnover. The ability to stop also provides a margin of safety for all players, regardless of age. As with starting, players must learn to control their skate edges to ensure quick and controlled stops during a game. Let's examine the two key elements associated with stopping in hockey.

Key Elements:

1. Two-foot stop, or "hockey stop"
2. One-foot stop

Two-Foot Stop, or Hockey Stop

This is the stop hockey players most commonly use. The lower body plays the key role in ensuring proper mechanics. Because you must place all your weight over the balls of your feet to execute this stop, you must be able to maintain balance (figure 5.1). This is difficult for new players to master because it requires a commitment to balance and edge control.

You will undoubtedly have a "strong" side for stopping, finding it easier to stop facing either to your left or right side. Realize that you must practice stopping drills to both sides because you need to be proficient in either direction during game situations. In the hockey stop you must stay low by bending your knees and ankles so they can act as shock absorbers as the stop begins. This will assist you in maintaining

Figure 5.1   Proper stopping balance for the two-foot stop

your weight over the balls of your feet. Keep the skates in a heel-to-toe spacing, positioning the heel area of your front skate slightly in front of the toe of your other skate (figure 5.2). This formation provides sound weight distribution across both skate blades. You will notice that you use the outside edge of the inside skate blade. The lead skate will see the inside edge cutting the ice.

During a game a player must often stop suddenly to prevent or reduce contact with an opponent. The upper body must therefore be under control during the hockey stop to prepare for contact and so avoid uncomfortable situations. Similarly, when in possession of the puck a quick two-footed stop can allow you to change direction and deceive an opponent as you make your way to the net. In either situation, you should position the upper body over the inside skate to maximize balance and stability during a stopping sequence.

Common Problems

• Be careful not to allow your body to come over the top of the skate edges. Leaning too far forward will cause you to fall. Leaning forward just a little will cause you to slide backwards.

Figure 5.2 Proper heel alignment for stopping

Both situations are a common occurrence for players just learning edge control. The corrective drill is 18.

• Avoid spreading your legs too far apart or positioning them too close together. Try to keep your feet in a heel-to-toe relationship, approximately shoulder-width apart. The corrective drill is 20.

• If you witness your blades chattering as the stop occurs, it normally means that your weight distribution is too far toward the heel areas. Corrective drills are 19 and 20.

• Focus your eyes in the direction you want to travel when you complete the stop. This will ensure that the head turns first, which will help lead the body toward your intended target area. Corrective drills are 20 and 21.

• Do not dip the shoulders while stopping. Try to keep them level to the ice surface when possible. This helps with overall balance and is especially important in maintaining puck control. Corrective drills are 19, 20, and 21.

• In open-ice situations without possession of the puck keep only one hand on the stick and use this to help you turn off a sudden stop as required. The corrective drill is 19.

• Maintain a strong knee-bend position throughout the stop. After virtually every stop a start begins your momentum again, which means that you need good knee bend to push off in the other direction. Stay low as you complete the stop by bending the knees close to 90 degrees. Corrective drills are 19 and 20.

One-Foot Stop

As you develop more confidence in stopping, the one-foot stop will become another option. This stop requires tremendous confidence in your edge control because all your body weight will be focused on one blade, centered on either the outside or inside edge depending on which one-foot stop you use. This stop allows players to shift their weight quickly in another direction, decreasing the time required to change direction. Mastering this stop requires practice and great body awareness.

In a one-foot stop your body weight moves over the foot that is stopping. You must bend this leg close to 90 degrees to maximize efficiency in the stop. The other skate blade is close to the ice surface and, in preparation for a turn or quick movement, down and into the ice as you make the stop. Figure 5.3 shows a one-foot stop that incorporates the inside edge of the stopping skate. Notice the difference between that stop and a one-foot stop that uses primarily the outside edge of the stop skate, shown figure in 5.4. The latter is not as efficient because more recovery time is required when using the off-ice skate. Also, skaters find it more difficult to maintain balance when using this style. Make sure that your upper body does not get too far forward over the front or toes of the stopping skate because this will result in a poor stop or possibly a fall.

When executing a one-foot stop all the body weight shifts toward a single edge located on one skate blade. With so much pressure being forced onto one contact point, it is vital that you distribute your weight over the ball of the foot. Just as in the two-footed stop, you must position the upper body over the stopping skate. Keep your head up and your eyes looking in the direction to which you next intend to move. As the stop begins you should keep your shoulders level and prepare to open

Figure 5.3 One-foot stop on inside edge of stopping skate

Figure 5.4   One-foot stop on outside edge of stopping skate

them toward the intended direction of travel. Also, try to envision your back staying relatively straight throughout this stop, which will help achieve solid weight distribution. Finally, have your stick in one hand only and close to the ice, ready to move toward the next target area as you complete the stop.

Common Problems

• If you do not bend the stopping leg properly, your weight will be located too far toward the heel area. The corrective drill is 18.

• If you do not distribute your body weight over the ball of the foot and on the correct edge, your ankle may turn over. This will cause a poor stop or even a crash landing on the ice. Corrective drills are 18 and 19.

• As with the two-footed stop, do not focus your eyes down and into the ice but up and toward your next destination. The corrective drill is 18.

- If poor balance is evident watch shoulder location as the stop begins. Players often have their shoulders too far forward, which contributes to poor balance. The corrective drill is 21.

Skate-Print Analysis for Effective Stops

Using skate prints to assess stopping mechanics is similar in principle to the technique used in the previous chapter to assess starting technique. Here too you can use a partner to help you determine whether you are properly executing your hockey stop or one-footed stop. Have a clean portion of the ice available just as you did for the starting section. Practice stopping actions to see both the direction and length of your individual stopping sequence. An ideal two-footed stop will have ice marks that look similar to those found in figure 5.5. Notice that the marks are in a straight line, meaning that the weight distribution was over the balls of the feet and both edges were used properly. Also, the marks begin narrow and become wider as the stop finishes. Obviously, the quicker the stop the faster the next start, which translates into an increase in quickness.

Now look at the marks in figure 5.6. You'll see that the stop faded to one side and the total stopping sequence covered a considerably longer distance than the one in the previous figure. These types of marks will indicate any number of problems, from poor weight distribution to improper heel-to-toe alignment. Try this activity to learn more about your strengths and weaknesses in stopping across both key elements. Coaches will find that players enjoy these types of learning experiences.

Summary

Learning how to stop effectively goes beyond the simple safety concerns that make it an essential skill for all hockey players. The modern game requires players who can stop on a dime. Many coaches identify stopping with the special-teams realm of penalty killing. To compete when short handed, players must be able to cut down the passing and shooting angles that the opponent will attempt to exploit. The ability to do this

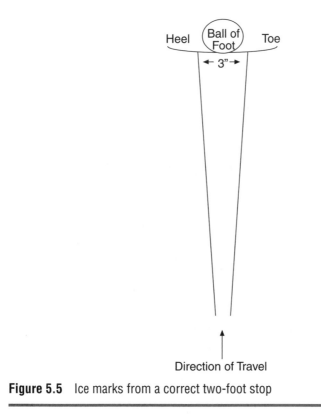

Figure 5.5 Ice marks from a correct two-foot stop

relates directly to players' skill at stopping and starting while under pressure. Players who can master the quick stop soon find that their coach will have need for their skill many times during a match. Of course, sometimes the same coach will yell out for transition, a concept that relates to starting and stopping as well as the next topic we examine in this book, namely *turning.*

Drill Section Notes

Consider the following information while attempting the stopping drills in this chapter. First, in any drill that runs the length of the ice you should always practice stopping toward the same side of the rink all the way down and back. This ensures that you will be stopping on both sides of your skates using all edges. Many younger players will stop only toward

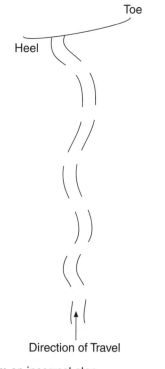

Figure 5.6   Ice marks from an incorrect stop

their strong side because they feel more confident and comfortable. You should realize that stopping is not always convenient during a game, so use the drills in this section to practice your stopping proficiency both ways.

Second, we have included only a few stopping drills because you can incorporate a stopping action at the end of almost any hockey activity. Therefore, use some of the other drills in this book to reinforce both your one-foot and two-foot skating stops.

Finally, try to focus on balance points as you practice stopping. The most common problems associated with stopping are related to poor balance. So remember to avoid having (1) weight too far toward the heels, (2) shoulders too far forward, and (3) not enough knee bend. It is easy to become too concerned with the lower body because this is where all the action appears to take place. By incorporating proper upper-body positioning, however, you will find that the lower body can do its job much more easily. Keeping your body in balance will greatly enhance your ability to stop correctly and quickly.

18 ZIGZAG

Purpose

To reinforce proper edge control of both skates while stopping.

Procedure

1. Divide players into four groups of equal size, each group using one-quarter of the ice surface.
2. Place pylons in zigzag formation 10 to 15 feet apart as illustrated (photo a).
3. Players begin by skating toward the first pylon and stop by using only the inside edge of one skate (photo b). They then continue to the next pylon, again using only an inside edge of the opposite skate to stop (photo c).
4. After players stop at each pylon they return to their original locations and complete the course again, this time using only outside edges to stop. To complete the drill, players use the two-footed stop at each pylon.

Key Points

• You should keep your weight over the balls of your stopping foot regardless of the edge you use.

• Sound knee and ankle bend is vital, with the knee positioned toward the front of the skate at each stop location.

• In one-footed stops, your upper body should be entirely over the stop skate. In two-footed stops, your upper body will be in a line over the inside skate only.

(a)

(b)

(c)

19 LEFT- AND RIGHT-FOOT STOPS

Purpose

To practice preparation for change of direction off a stop by using a 180-degree body rotation.

Procedure

1. The drill can work using either line markings on the ice or a coach's commands.
2. Players begin by skating in a straight line followed by a stop on the inside edge of either the left or right skate (photo a).
3. At the conclusion of the stop the body should be facing in a different direction, with the skates set in a V-start position. Players complete the drill by initiating a start.

Key Points

• Remember that every stop in hockey leads to another start, so proper body positioning is vital.

• If players execute the stop correctly, they are able to view sooner more of the ice surface as they are stopping.

• This drill should be done in open ice, away from traffic.

• Note that the skater in photo b has not completed a full 180-degree rotation.

LEFT- AND RIGHT-FOOT STOPS

(a)

(b)

SKIING

Purpose

As a lead-up drill for the hockey, or two-foot, stop.

Procedure

1. Players begin by skating forward to generate speed, followed by a glide with both feet close together under the body (photo a).
2. Players then attempt to make a 90-degree rotation of the body by unweighting the heels of both skates while rotating the upper body (photo b).
3. Players repeat this action over the length of the ice.

Key Points

• To rotate to the left you should tip both skates slightly to the left to get onto the proper edge. The same applies when attempting to rotate and stop in the opposite direction.

• Your weight should be over the balls of your feet as you attempt this maneuver.

• If your weight falls back toward your heels, you will either effect a turn rather than a stop, or your skates will chatter, indicating that you have completed a poor stop.

(a)

(b)

PARTNER PULL

Purpose

To practice both starting and stopping technique with resistance.

Procedure

1. Players skate with a partner. Each takes a turn being the player who is pulled and then being the one who does the pulling.
2. The pulling player takes hold of both stick blades while the player being pulled holds on to the butt ends of both sticks (photo a).
3. The puller attempts to skate with his or her partner the length of the ice (photo b).
4. As players reach each line, blue then red then blue, the back player attempts to stop and offers resistance.
5. Players switch positions after they have completed a full length of the ice.

Key Points

• Always keep the toes of the stick blades facing down toward the ice to prevent an injury in case of a fall.

• The back player can offer additional resistance before each line to force the puller to work harder during the activity.

• Both players should concentrate on staying bent at the knees during this drill.

• This activity can be attempted with the puller skating backward as pictured, or with both players skating forward.

(a)

(b)

Turning

Imagine yourself skating effortlessly toward the opposition net, puck well positioned on the stick blade, the enemy goaltender coming closer by the second. Just as you prepare to unleash the goal-scoring shot, a pesky back-checker somehow picks your pocket clean. You are suddenly faced with the task of changing direction and becoming an attacker rather than a defender. Or perhaps you are battling along the sideboards in the opposition's end with a player hotly in pursuit and well positioned to stop your efforts at attacking the net. You execute a quick turn. Before anyone can react, you skate toward the net and unleash a kill shot for a crucial goal.

Certainly, these kinds of situations occur on almost a shift-to-shift basis during a hockey game. Just as surely players must be able to turn quickly during the heat of battle to maintain or regain possession of the puck. Many players have learned to use turning as a key element in their skating arsenal, and none does it better than the Great One himself, Wayne Gretzky. Although not blessed with tremendous physical attributes or blazing speed, Gretzky has learned to effect tight turns as an important aspect of his offensive game. His dedication to refining the "escape move," or tight turn, has allowed him to create space and time on the ice. Gretzky's use of turning is unparalleled and example enough of the impact that effective turning can have in a game. The speed associated with modern hockey requires players to develop skating techniques that will allow them to compete at higher tempos. The ability to turn quickly is especially evident during the transitional portions of a contest. Those who cannot keep up are often left in a sudden cloud of enemy ice chips!

In this chapter we will teach you how to improve your turning so that you can actually gain speed after executing this skill, rather than lose speed. We will examine three major types of turns in this section.

Key Elements:

1. Crossover turn
2. Glide turn
3. Power turn

Crossover Turn

This is arguably the most difficult skating skill to master. The crossover turn is so named because its initiation requires continuous crossing action of the legs (figure 6.1). This is the most common turning action that many players use to change direction during a skating sequence. Properly executed, crossover turns can increase speed out of a turn, allowing a player to move in another direction without any loss of momentum.

It is important to understand that in this turn you do not distribute your weight to the same parts of both skate blades. Rather, you should exert pressure on the inside skate toward the heel and on the outside edge. On the crossing or stepping skate you should have most of your weight on the ball of the foot and located on the inside blade edge.

We have noted earlier in this book that the crossing action should occur in front of the support leg, not high and over the top. This allows you to keep your skates closer to the ice in preparation for the next phase of skating. Your knees must stay bent and close to 90 degrees to maximize power from the leg action in this turn. You must focus on pushing off both the inside skate and the crossing skate if you are to generate maximum speed out of the turn.

Although the lower body is the power plant for the crossover turn, the upper body acts as a balancing agent to help skaters realize maximum effectiveness in the turn. As previously

(b)

Figure 6.1 The crossover turn

reviewed in the chapters on starting and stopping, you should focus on a target up, not down, so that the knees remain bent and properly positioned. Crossover turning is often required when you must get quickly into transition, with or without the puck. You must position the upper body to accommodate any sudden change in game conditions. Keep your stick located in the direction of the intended turn to facilitate a quick transition. Shoulders should remain parallel to the ice and open to the side to which you are turning. The head should be up and the eyes looking back over the inside shoulder. For this or any other turn, your entire body must line up over your support, or glide, skate for optimum balance. As with all skating technique, this particular maneuver requires continual practice and a commitment to improving balance and edge control.

Common Problems

• Try to ensure that the outside foot crosses around the front of the inside skate, not over the top. The latter will create a hopping effect, which costs speed and time. The corrective drill is 28.

• Remember to push off both skates. Otherwise, if you push off only with the outside skate, you lose power and speed. Corrective drills are 23, 27, and 28.

• If you do not distribute your weight on the blades as previously described, you will probably fall because you cannot hold the turn. Balance and edge control are crucial elements of crossover turning. Corrective drills are 23 and 28.

• Many players will dip their shoulders toward the inside, in the direction of the turn, which results in a loss of power and poor balance. In this position, a player can be easily knocked down or have the puck dislodged from the stick. The corrective drill is 27.

• If you fail to look over the inside shoulder as you make the turn, it will take longer to complete. Focus on snapping the chin toward your target area, and the rest of the body will follow. The corrective drill is 23.

Glide Turn

During a game you will at times want to conserve energy, concentrate on puck control, or focus on checking assignments. Performing these duties might be easier if you do not use a crossover turn. The glide turn allows you to concentrate on other tasks without worrying about high-tempo skating technique (figure 6.2).

As the name implies, players simply glide through this turn rather than skate through it. The player who performs this turn while carrying the puck can bear down on a defender or opposition goalie. Balance is a key to proper glide-turn execution. To maintain it, the lower body must remain relatively still. As always, try to keep your knees bent to 90 degrees and space the skates approximately shoulder-width apart. The exact distance of separation between the two skates will vary depending on the severity of the turn angle, the strength of the player turning, and individual comfort levels.

You should not push your skates during the actual turn phase; instead maintain contact with the ice throughout the turn sequence. Realize that the inside skate leads you through this turn. You should distribute your weight to the outside edge of the lead skate and the inside edge of the trailing skate, with body weight toward the heels of both skates.

Part of the advantage of using a glide turn is that it frees the upper body for other aspects of play. A glide turn is often the turn of choice when controlling a puck. This allows you to focus on maintaining control while easily changing direction. Remember that the stick should always be close to the ice in a glide turn, with or without the puck, because proper stick location will help you turn with greater ease and efficiency. Keep your arms and hands extended from your body, allowing you to carry the puck with less risk of losing it in your skates. Having the arms away from the hips will also make it easier to complete a checking assignment away from the puck because your arms are positioned to attack. Remember that your shoulders should be level, as with all turns or stops, to achieve maximum balance. This is especially important when carrying the puck. Also, you should initiate the turn with a head-and-shoulder rotation, which will open up your hips and legs to follow.

(a)

(b)

Figure 6.2 The glide turn

Common Problems

• Try to avoid leaning too far forward or being too upright as you enter the turn. Either extreme will result in a poor glide technique and a loss of balance. Corrective drills are 22 and 25.

• If you spread your legs too far apart the recovery into the next skating sequence will be more difficult. Practice glide turns so that you can easily initiate the next explosive skating sequence after you complete the glide. The corrective drill is 22.

• Use glide turns selectively. If you can use only this type of turn, your game speed will suffer. Corrective drills are 23, 26, 27, and 28.

Power Turn

This is a little-known, seldom taught turning skill that can greatly affect your turning speed. Players normally use the dynamics of this turn at the completion of a glide turn. The upper- and lower-body dynamics for both are the same with one exception. In a power turn the ankle comes into play in a manner that is different from the way it is used in the glide turn (figure 6.3).

This turn requires great strength and even greater commitment to technique, especially during game situations. Skilled players, as they complete the glide turn, can use a power turn to give a sudden boost of speed to their next skating sequence. You accomplish this by applying pressure downward to the heel portion of the trailing skate and then snap the ankle joint. This will result in a C-cut action from the inside of your skate edge, which increases speed out of the turn.

Common Problems

• Do not confuse the C-cutting motion from the heel of the blade with a total weight distribution to the back portion of the trailing leg. The latter will result in poor balance and a loss of speed. The corrective drill is 26.

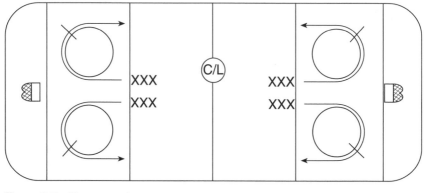

Figure 6.3　The power turn

• Timing is essential. You should attempt to initiate the power turn when the toes of both skates are facing the direction you intend to travel. Beginning the power turn too soon will accelerate you into the turn rather than out of the turn, while starting too late will result in minimal speed enhancement. The corrective drill is 26.

Summary

Of all the skating skills and techniques used in modern hockey, none is more important than the ability to turn quickly during play, especially at high speed. With the emphasis clearly shifting to a higher-tempo skill game, turning has become a benchmark on which many coaches make player personnel decisions. By practicing the drills in this chapter players will find over the long term that it takes less effort and time to execute tight turns. They will be able to execute escape moves more easily at higher speeds, with or without the puck. These kinds of skills will enable a player to progress through the hockey ranks and compete at the highest levels of the game.

Drill Section Notes

The seven drills in this section will help you develop all the skills associated with crossover, glide, and power turns. Turning is a difficult skill to master. Although strength is a key for all skating mechanics, technique is even more important in developing fluid and effective turn moves. Attempt first to understand each turning action as you slowly work your way through each drill. Some of the activities are designed for work with a partner. You can include resistance to add a conditioning factor. Your ultimate goal should be to complete all the drills at top-end speed, even increasing your speed out of the turn when you use crossovers and power turns.

360-DEGREE TURNS

Purpose

A lead-up drill for learning the glide turn.

Procedure

1. Players may begin at either end of the rink in wave formation, using five lines.
2. At the coach's command, players in the first group skate forward to gain momentum and then begin to glide on the flats of their skate edges.
3. At the near blue line, with skates positioned shoulder-width apart and shoulders parallel to the ice, players open their upper bodies toward either the left or right side, following the coach's instructions (see diagram).
4. Players then rotate the shoulders fully in the direction of the turn while both skates lean in that direction. Players shift body weight toward the heel areas of both skates.
5. Players then hold for a 360-degree glide turn and repeat the activity at the next blue line.

Key Points

• If you do not shift your weight to the heels, you will slow nearly to a standstill before you complete the turn.

• The purpose here is to practice the glide and edge control, so do not snap the head quickly to make the turn faster. You should execute a wide glide turn in this drill.

• Listen to the coach for a command or watch for the direction in which the coach tells you to turn. If only one player turns in the wrong direction you are liable to make contact with another player.

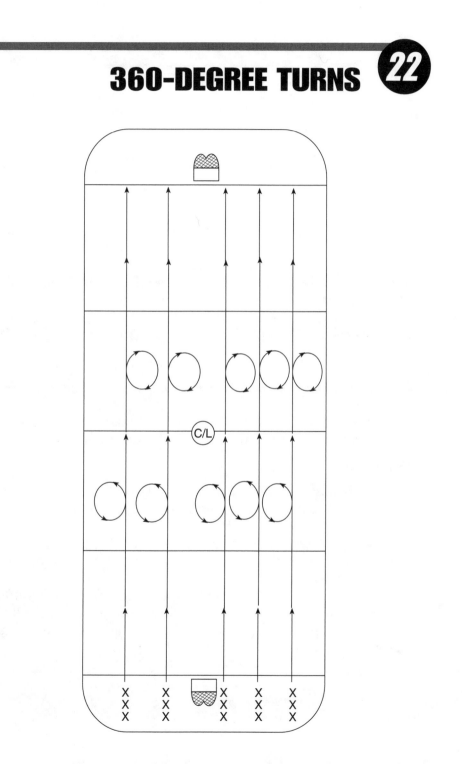

FIGURE 8

Purpose

A lead-up drill for crossover turns, practicing outside edge control.

Procedure

1. Players move to an open location anywhere on the ice surface, making sure to allow ample space between team-mates to execute the drill.
2. On their own time players begin a figure-8 skating pattern. Players attempt an alternate glide motion on one side of the 8 using the outside edge of the left skate, and use the left outside edge at the other end of the figure-8 loop (see diagram).
3. As they begin each turn, players should weight the heel area of the glide skate as they did in the previous drill.
4. Once the drill begins players keep their sticks in the proper hand, the top hand, with the stick always pointed toward the center area of the figure 8.

Key Points

- Try to keep your shoulders parallel to the ice, never allowing them to dip. Only your knees should be bending during this exercise.
- Have your body weight positioned over the glide skate, not leaning too far toward the inside or outside of the loop you are skating.
- If you find yourself having trouble completing this circuit, you might have your weight too far forward. This may result in your skate digging in the ice and beginning to slide, or your ankle rolling over, causing you to stop.

FIGURE 8 **23**

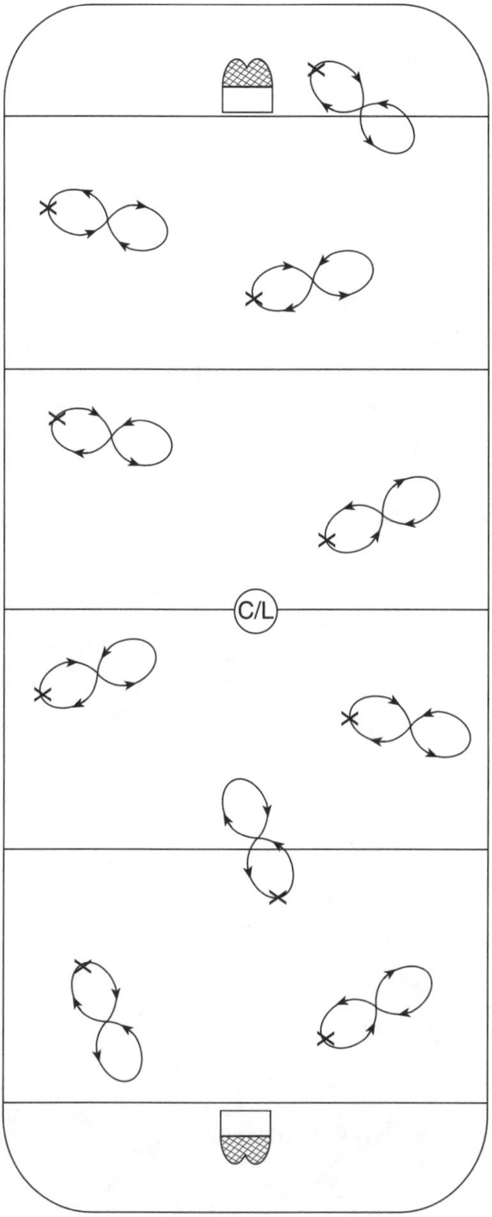

SLALOM

Purpose

To practice edge control and proper blade positioning for the lead skate.

Procedure

1. Divide players into four equal groups, placing a group in each corner of the rink.
2. Set up in a straight line a series of 10 or fewer pylons.
3. On the coach's whistle, players skate out in single file and position their skates as if beginning a skiing pattern. Players should have skates close together in a heel-to-toe relationship as they reach the first pylon.
4. Players stop skating and focus on slaloming through the pylons without stopping, allowing the inside skate to lead them though each turn.

Key Points

• This is an excellent lead-up drill for either the glide or crossover because it forces you to work on efficient blade positioning.

• You must shift your weight toward the heels as you begin to slalom.

• Shift your shoulders over the inside skate at each pylon to effect the turn.

• Concentrate on tipping your ankles slightly to either the left or right, depending on the side to which you are turning, and let your edges do the work.

25 AIRPLANE

Purpose

To reinforce proper upper-body positioning during a glide turn.

Procedure

1. Assemble players in waves or put them in groups within the three zones of the ice surface.
2. Players in one group skate forward while keeping their sticks rested on their shoulders, clasped in both hands (photo a).
3. As the players move forward they open the shoulders toward the side to which they intend to turn. Players execute a glide turn, either 180 or 360 degrees, depending on the coach's preference (photo b).
4. Once the first group completes a turn, the next group of players begins.

Key Points

• You are attempting to do a tight glide turn in this drill so you must rotate the upper body toward the side to which you are turning. This will shorten the turn radius.

• As mentioned in previous drills, it is important that you do not dip your shoulders excessively in either direction. You will notice your stick leaving the position parallel to the ice if you dip your shoulders.

• This drill demonstrates how quickly you can execute a glide turn by leading the upper-body rotation into the turn with the chin and shoulders.

(a)

(b)

CLOCK DRILL

Purpose

As a lead-up drill for the proper execution of a power turn.

Procedure

1. Put players in groups around the many face-off circles on the ice surface, or put a marker on the ice (for example, a glove) to simulate a face-off circle.
2. In single file and at the coach's command, players skate to the face-off dot or marker and begin a glide turn at a controlled speed (photo a).
3. Depending on whether they are moving right or left, the players initiate a snap at the ankle joint at the five o'clock or seven o'clock areas on the circle. Players make the C-cut from the inside edge of the skate blade (photo b).
4. Once the players come out of the turn, they go to the back of their group and try the drill again in the opposite direction.

Key Points

• It is difficult to discipline yourself to wait until you have reached the five o'clock or seven o'clock position before making a forward C-cut with your skate. If you execute the C-cut from the heel of the outside skate too soon, however, you will lose the turn radius. If you wait too long you will lose any acceleration effect.

• Executing the C-cut at precisely the right moment will increase your speed out of the glide turn.

• This drill requires the same positioning as a basic glide turn. Have your weight back on your heels and push off the inside edge of the push leg at just the right moment.

(a)

(b)

PARTNER CIRCLE

Purpose

To use face-off circles in practicing crossover turns while using resistance.

Procedure

1. Pair up players at any of the many face-off circles on the ice surface.
2. A pair of players enters the circle (photo a). One skater attempts to practice crossover turns. The partner takes a position just inside the circle line within arm's reach of his or her partner (photo b).
3. At the coach's whistle, the players begin skating with the inside partner attempting to push the outside partner off the crossover path (photo c).
4. After approximately 20 seconds players switch roles and attempt the drill again.

Key Points

• Remember to try this activity both clockwise and counter-clockwise to develop crossovers in both directions.

• The inside skater should offer resistance appropriate to the skill level of the partner.

• This activity will reinforce the importance of keeping shoulders parallel to the ice. Any dipping will result in poor balance and an inability to complete the drill.

• You can start this activity without a stick, then add a stick for both players, and finally try it with a puck on the stick of the player attempting the crossover technique.

(a)

(b)

(c)

28 SCULLING CIRCLE

Purpose

To practice edge control as a lead-up to the crossover turn.

Procedure

1. Players form groups at either end and use the end-zone face-off circles. Another group may use the neutral zone if pylons are placed to designate a turning location.
2. Players move forward in single file. As they approach a circle they begin to push with only their outside skate from the heel, executing C-cuts as they make their way around the circle (photo a).
3. After they complete the first circle and skate halfway to the other circle, the players switch to sculling with the other skate, using the other blade to move in the opposite direction around a second face-off circle (photos b and c).
4. The drill continues until the coach stops it.

Key Points

• It is vital that you keep the weight of your nonsculling, or support, leg toward your heel and primarily over the outside edge as you make your way through the turn.

• You should position your upper body over the support leg for better balance and keep your shoulders parallel to the ice surface.

• The amount of heel weighting you employ will depend on the severity of the turn you wish to execute.

• Also, tip both skates to the side to which you wish to travel, using the inside edge of the sculling skate and the outside edge of the support leg.

(a)

(b)

(c)

Pivoting

The puck has just been shot into the neutral zone. You must quickly retrieve it and look for an open teammate to start a transition play. As you near the puck your body is facing your defensive zone, not the ideal position for launching an offensive attack. Suddenly, you pivot from forward skating to backward, your skates churning the ice as you buy time and space waiting for your linemate to get open.

In this common game situation, proper pivoting technique allows you to maintain puck control while gaining better position on the ice. Many current professionals have mastered this move to their advantage, especially defensemen. Players such as Brian Leetch and Ray Bourque have made pivoting a vital part of their games, a skill that allows them to move almost instantly from defense to offense. Pivoting is an integral part of modern hockey.

Pivoting while skating is a skill closely related to turning. It is often thought of as a semiturn, in which a player moves from skating forward to backward or vice versa. This skill is especially important in defending against an attacker or as a means of eluding an opponent when in control of the puck. As with other skating skills, players must first understand the mechanics of the action, especially at high speed while attempting to control a puck. In this chapter we will examine two key elements associated with proper pivoting technique.

Key Elements:

1. Mohawk
2. Crossover

Mohawk

Pivoting, as opposed to turning, allows a player to change from forward to backward skating or backward to forward without having to change direction. This is often a 180-degree change rather than a full 360-degree turn. Pivoting is an especially important skill for the transition portion of the game. Quick feet and lower-body control are key aspects of proper pivoting technique.

To initiate the Mohawk pivot from forward to backward skating, rotate both the head and shoulder areas toward the direction you ultimately want to face at the conclusion of the pivot. At the same time, rotate your glide leg approximately 90 degrees and transfer your weight to the opposite skate, placing the skate boot close to the heel of the glide skate in an L or T shape. A momentary gliding action occurs on one skate while you raise the other slightly off the ice. When attempting to move from forward to backward you will be completing a half turn. Try to keep the flats of both skates in a position to accept your body weight in and out of the maneuver.

When moving from backward to forward you must again initiate the move by rotating both your head and shoulders toward your intended direction of travel (figure 7.1). At the same time, open the hip by placing your skate heels close together, with the toe of your stepping skate pointed toward the intended direction of travel. Your body line and weight must be over the glide leg as you pick up the stepping foot to make the pivot, making sure to distribute your weight over the ball of the foot. As the hip opens, transfer your weight onto the stepping skate. Your first full stride should be made with your initial stepping skate off the inside edge of the blade.

Common Problems

- Often players will not commit to gliding on one foot before they attempt the pivot. As their balance improves, players will

(a)

(b)

(c)

Figure 7.1 The mohawk pivot

find this transition easier to complete. The corrective drill is 29.

• Players should avoid hopping or jumping in the air as they attempt to pivot. Both skates should always be either on the ice or very close to the ice surface during any pivoting action. The corrective drill is 31.

• Often a player will forget to rotate the head and shoulder to begin the pivot, resulting in poor balance and often a loss of speed. The corrective drill is 30.

Crossover

By this juncture of the book you should be familiar with crossover principles. We have used this concept in forward skating, backward skating, and starting. Most of the important principles of crossover maneuvers previously noted apply to pivoting. The key to this skill is that your stride skate must cross in front of your support, or glide, skate under the midline of the body so that you can transfer your body weight to that skate (figure 7.2). You then follow the same procedures that we outlined for the Mohawk. Remember, do not extend your crossover foot too high in the air because doing so will reduce overall speed. Players use this move more often when pivoting from backward to forward skating. Stronger, more advanced skaters should attempt the crossover. Much like the crossover start, your outside leg will stride in front of the support leg to initiate the pivot.

Summary

We have now moved through most of the key hockey skating skills that players and coaches should know. It is time to provide a general framework that will help you use effectively the drills and ideas in practice and game situations. The next chapter in the book will clarify ways to achieve this as we present some principles for practice.

Figure 7.2 The crossover pivot

Drill Section Notes

The three pivoting activities in this section will slow you down so that you can walk through the technique side of pivoting. When you have mastered the basics, try the drills at high speed and you will understand what a difficult skill pivoting is to master. You will undoubtedly prefer one method over the other, and you will probably find it easier to pivot forward to backward or perhaps vice versa. But as with all other skating elements you must become competent at all aspects of pivoting. A key in any pivoting or turning action is to lead with the chin; the rest of your body will follow.

FOUR-STEP COMMAND

Purpose

As a lead-up drill to practice the Mohawk pivot.

Procedure

1. Players begin with their backs facing their intended direction of travel. Players should initially do this drill at walking pace, not at speed.
2. When the coach says "Look," players initiate the move by rotating the head and shoulder areas (photo a).
3. When the coach says "Quarter turn," players rotate the support, or glide, skate 90 degrees while opening their hips in the intended direction of travel (photo b).
4. As the coach says "Step," players load up their support leg and transfer their weight onto the stepping skate, which is pointed in the intended direction of travel.
5. Finally, the coach says "Go," and players finish the activity by taking three powerful strides.

Key Points

• Keep the stick in only one hand during this drill and make sure you have it pointed in the direction to which you are rotating the shoulders and head.

• Try to have your head and shoulders positioned over the support leg while executing the rotation. This will give you better balance and power.

• By rotating your head and shoulders to your intended direction of travel, you will be positioned to complete the quarter pivot on the glide, or support, skate. Position the stepping skate so that the toe is pointing toward your intended line of travel.

FOUR-STEP COMMAND 29

(a)

(b)

133

③⓪ ALTERNATING 180S

Purpose

To develop foot speed and quickness while maintaining balance and control during pivoting.

Procedure

1. Players line up along the goal line at one end of the rink in a wave formation (six lines).
2. Players in the first group skate forward and on the coach's whistle quickly pivot 180 degrees to a backward-skating position (photos a and b).
3. On the next whistle, players pivot back to forward (photo c).
4. The drill continues until the players reach the end of the ice, when another wave skates forward to continue the activity.

Key Points

• You should attempt both the Mohawk and crossover pivot during this drill.

• You should practice pivoting to both sides, so alternate your turns.

• As you gain technical ability, attempt to execute these pivots at high speed, forcing yourself to keep good balance while working on your overall quickness.

• Remember at the pivot point to rotate your head and shoulders toward your intended direction of travel.

(a)

(b)

(c)

FOUR CORNERS

Purpose

To reinforce proper technique using either type of pivot.

Procedure

1. Players are in one of four groups located at one of the four face-off dots just outside the blue lines.
2. In single file, players in one group skate forward toward the top of the face-off circle near the goal line and execute a pivot from forward to backward (see diagram). The players then skate toward the goal line, pivot forward, turn, and skate back out to the blue line.
3. All players go to the opposite line from where they began outside the blue line, and the next group of skaters moves forward in the other direction.

Key Points

• This simple activity will test your ability to pivot to both sides.

• As your pivoting skill improves you will want to include pucks in this activity.

• Remember to keep your upper body in good position over your support leg before attempting to pivot.

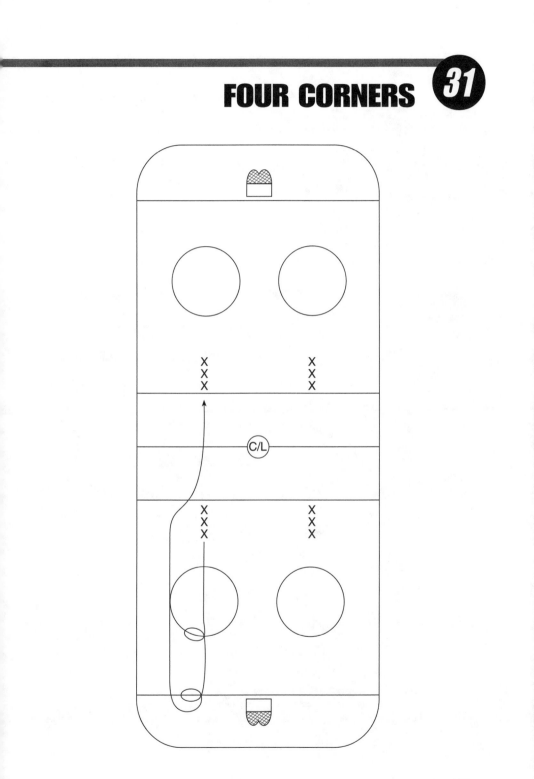

Principles
of Practice

As in any sport, effective and efficient hockey practice requires considerable planning and preparation. To learn the many components of skating, you must develop the practice techniques that will give you the most return on your time and energy. With that in mind, this chapter will provide players and coaches alike useful tools to use during practice sessions. Given swelling numbers of participants and increasing ice-time costs, the tips found here will be valuable from both a developmental and financial perspective. Specifically, we will examine the following:

1. Start by drilling slowly to ensure a measure of success through proper technique.
2. Use multiple zones for practice sessions.
3. Incorporate waves or lines in drilling.
4. Enhance all drills to include specific skating components.
5. Include innovative and enjoyable activities.

Start by Drilling Slowly

Learning how to skate properly can be frustrating. The beginner must come to grips with such variables as balance points and edge control. The task can seem daunting. More experienced players will have another problem to contend with, namely undoing poor technique that they have learned and that has been reinforced, perhaps over many years.

In either case, when working on a difficult skill you should not hesitate to begin the drill sequence with a walk-through approach. This means that players will be stationary to begin the activity and then attempt the skill while walking at a slow speed. After players understand and can demonstrate the proper technique, it is time to put the drill in motion.

You may wish to structure an activity to include stations directed to different levels of ability within a given skill set. Players may then choose their own entry and exit points. This system can make players more comfortable, especially those who might initially have trouble keeping up. As previously noted, you must learn to walk before you can skate, and walking on the ice to reinforce a skill set reflects sound teaching principles.

Use Multiple Zones for Practice Sessions

Historically, coaches paid little attention to practice format, to the way they organized and executed a typical practice period. But with an ever-increasing number of players and with facilities booked to the brim, it has become important for coaches and players to use practice sessions efficiently. One way to maximize the value of ice time is to distribute players into groups at different locations around the ice surface, with each group involved in a different activity.

Perhaps the simplest way to break a full team into smaller groups is by using the natural boundaries already outlined on the ice surface. One group would work in one end zone, defined as the area from the blue line to the end boards. A second group would occupy the neutral-zone area between the two blue lines, while a third group of players might practice at the other end of the rink (see figure 8.1). This format allows the coach to run three distinct groups and activities simultaneously, which means that players will receive more repetitions and practice time rather than waiting in line in a large group.

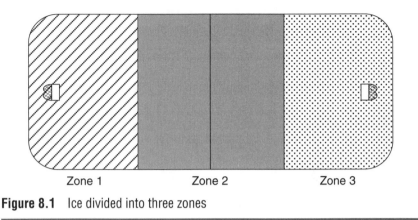

Figure 8.1 Ice divided into three zones

Another approach to doing group work in practice is to divide the ice into thirds going the length of the ice (see figure 8.2). You can do this by placing pylons every 5 to 10 feet to outline the different zones. Make sure that players understand the importance of staying in their zone during skating activities to avoid contact with other skaters.

Many minor hockey associations now schedule two teams for the same ice surface during practice sessions, especially with younger age groups. In this type of format you might consider station work to maximize ice use. Put players in pairs or small groups at different locations and provide various activities for a specific skill set in skating. After three minutes each pair or group will rotate to another station (see figure 8.3). Although this system of practice requires some initial start-up

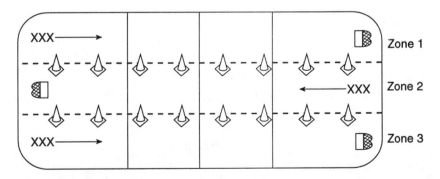

Figure 8.2 Ice divided into three zones lengthwise using pylons

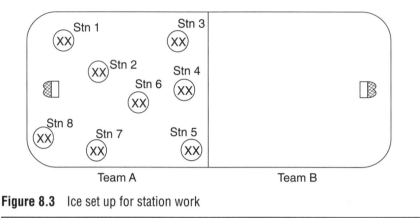

Figure 8.3　Ice set up for station work

explanation and organization, players will soon come to understand the format and you will be able to accomplish a great deal with limited space and time.

Unfortunately, it is all too common to witness practice sessions in which 18 or 20 players stand and watch one or two players complete an activity. This fails to develop the majority of players and is a costly and poor use of ice time. Whether your preference is two, three, four, or even more groups of players, dividing the ice for group work makes sense. Certainly the number of coaches available and the type of activity you want to run will determine the number of groups you can use.

Use a Wave Formation in Drilling

Over the years Huron instructors have often found themselves on the ice with groups of players whose numbers exceed a normal team complement. This often occurs at a clinic presentation or hockey school location, and coaches must be able to accommodate these large numbers efficiently. One way to accomplish this is to use a wave formation.

Using waves maximizes ice time for all participants while allowing individual players to practice specific skills or activities. A coach may assemble any number of lines or rows of players at one end of the ice surface and call out waves of players one group at a time to practice a skill (see figure 8.4).

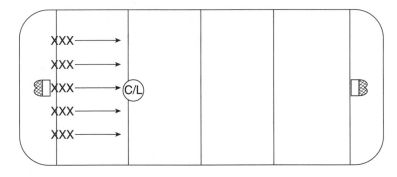

Figure 8.4 The wave formation

Players complete their wave and stay at the opposite end of the rink, waiting for their turn to head back in the other direction. This format allows coaches to maintain solid control over the players while providing a meaningful number of repetitions.

Using the three-zone format discussed in the previous section, you can break the players into smaller groups and have them practice skating skills going sideways across the ice in waves, rather than using the entire ice surface (see figure 8.5). Regardless of the format you use, you can use waves effectively for individual teams because you can run many drilling patterns through a wave format. Coaches will find this organizational tool helpful in reinforcing skill components.

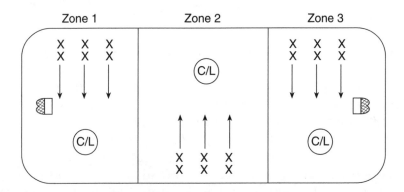

Figure 8.5 The three-zone wave formation

Include Specific Skating Components in All Drills

We all intuitively understand how important skating is to hockey. Yet often coaches and players will forget to reinforce fundamental skating skills in their drills or activities. For example, virtually any stationary activity run during practice can be revamped to include reinforcement of a skating skill. In addition, many drills that have been traditional mainstays for coaches and teams can be improved by creatively adding a skating component.

Let's assume, for example, that the coach of a pee-wee level team has designed a straight-ahead one-on-one drill between a forward and a defender. Often, the drill will begin when the coach blows a whistle and end when the puck is in the net or the goalie makes a save. To assist both players why not include a specific skating skill besides the straight-ahead component? Let's say that for the same one-on-one drill the coach asks all players to begin with a tight turn or pivot as the whistle sounds. This simple addition will obligate players to work on those specific skills, turning and pivoting, as well as straight-ahead skating. Or, instead of starting straight ahead, have the forward do a complete loop of the corner face-off circle while the defender does the same at the center circle, requiring both to improve their crossover skills. By beefing up the skating aspect of every drill run in practice, players and coaches can over time dramatically improve skating technique and efficiency.

Players may sometimes have to coach themselves to improve their skating technique and outcomes. Drills often end with a player shooting at a goalie, then skating back in line for another turn. Why not improve this drill yourself by incorporating finishing techniques that will improve the drill and your skill? Perhaps you will make a conscious effort to follow your shot to the net for any rebound opportunity and then stop or pivot toward the goal line as you make your way quickly to the back of the line. Adding a finishing aspect to your drills will enhance not only your skating but also your conditioning. After all, in the end, you are accountable for your skating development, so take charge in practice and make each activity count.

Include Innovative and Enjoyable Activities

Many players can recount horror stories of former coaches who made practice time drudgery because the content was always the same. Players soon memorized the drilling patterns, and practice became a chore. In today's world of video games and other high-tech, thrill-a-minute activities, we need to provide an environment to which players will want to return for more. While practice doesn't necessarily have to resemble a Super Mario experience, it should be enjoyable at least to the point where players want more. We suggest that coaches include a variety of new and unfamiliar objects and activities to reinforce skating while providing fun. For example, some coaches use balloons, ropes, parachutes, and other items to create entertaining activities that serve to improve skating. By including some drills that players are not familiar with, the coach can heighten interest and often reinforce a skating skill without the players' even realizing it! Make having fun a principle of practice, and your players will respond positively.

Players can continue to upgrade their skating mechanics and technique by using these practice principles. The result will be a more efficient skating style. Realize, however, that mastering the difficult skills associated with skating takes much time and patience. With this in mind, as you use the principles described in this chapter you might also consider the following skating tips to aid overall development of your skating style. You will recognize some of this information as a review from previous portions of the book. It is important, however, that you continue to reinforce these ideas to make proper skating mechanics an inherent part of your game.

- *When using any of the skating drills in this book remember to attempt activities in more than one direction.* Most players will have a dominant leg, which means you will probably be able to execute activities better in one direction than another. For example, if you notice that you can cross over more effectively going to your left, try to develop the weaker side by practicing the drill in both directions. Hockey will not allow you to skate in only one direction, so to take your game to the next level you must be able to skate strongly to both the left or right in all skating-related activities. Become aware of your weaker side, and even if drills are not specifically designed to work in both directions, take the initiative to make sure both sides get the necessary work.

• *Learn to conserve your energy by maximizing each skating stride.* Try to get the greatest bang for your skating buck by fully extending each skating stroke, not only at the knee joint but also at the ankle. Once you are able to extend the legs fully your skating style will improve. You will thus conserve energy that you can use later in the contest when it could tip the outcome of the game. This must become a part of all your drilling. You consciously develop your quickness off the start and follow it with consistent full extension during the striding phase of all open-ice skating.

• *Finally, regardless of the type of activity or system of practice, try to stay bent close to 90 degrees in all your skating drills and activities.* This is a key for improvement because most of the power generated for skating originates in the big muscle groups of the lower body. By staying lower to the playing surface (bending the knees) players will activate these big muscles to perform at their explosive best. In addition, by staying lower for longer periods players will be better able to accept any contact that will occur during games. You will therefore spend more time skating and less time picking yourself up off the ice! Increasing knee bend by only a few degrees can have a dramatic impact on the stability and efficiency of your skating style. Remember also that being aware of your balance points and learning proper upper-body positioning for each skill is critical to your skating development and success.

By incorporating these principles and skating tips each day, you will feel and see positive results during your hockey season. Understand that you will improve your skating by using proper technique. You must focus on these ideas while practicing to effect change. Proper skating doesn't happen by magic!

A Word About Roller (In-Line) Skating

Finally, communities with warm-weather climates are logical locations in which to use roller or in-line skating to learn and develop ice-skating skills. Although roller skates do not completely simulate skating on ice, the activity has tremendous potential for players who need additional activities to refine their skating. The balance points, body alignment, and muscle groups that provide the bulk of power for ice-hockey skaters will be affected in a positive way by roller skating. We recommend that you try in-line roller skating as a complementary off-ice activity that will move you closer to skating mastery.

Skating Mastery

In hockey, efficient and proper skating isn't a sometime thing; it must be an all-the-time thing. Many former players, professional and otherwise, learn this truth too late in their careers. As you made your way through this book you have learned many concepts and principles that can improve your skating style. Now, let's put your new knowledge to the test.

In the pages that follow are some of the most demanding skating drills and activities ever designed. Skaters at even the highest skill levels will find that these drills test their mettle and challenge their skating technique and ability. From proper use of edges to mastering balance points, from controlling upper-body movement to producing lower-body power, these drills include a wide range of skating principles that will reflect your mastery of the various skills. When you are able to complete these activities consistently, you will be on your way to mastering the science of skating.

In addition, we recommend that you do work off ice, which will help you develop many of the important elements associated with proper skating. Balance, leg strength, and upper- and lower-body alignment make up a foundation that you can build away from the rink. If you truly wish to improve your skating, you may have to make the commitment to include work away from the rink. Ice hockey has only recently become popular in many communities across North America. In such locations the ice time necessary to develop solid skating mechanics may be limited. This makes the off-ice component of your development even more important.

Good luck and good skating!

RUSSIAN KIP, FORWARD AND BACKWARD

Purpose

To develop quickness, balance, and foot speed.

Procedure

1. Players assemble in a wave formation at one end of the rink. The first group begins by skating forward to gain momentum.
2. At the near blue line players bend into a full sitting position and glide temporarily on the flats of both skate edges.
3. They then attempt to extend both skates fully in front of their bodies, leaving the ice surface at the same time (photo a).
4. The players then quickly return the skates under their bodies and attempt to repeat the action to the other end of the rink (photo b).

Key Points

- To achieve master status, you should be able to do this drill both forward and backward. However, even a master falls sometimes. Unfortunately, you might end up like the skater in photo c.
- You should bend fully at the knee and ankle joints to get in the full sitting position, which is the best balance position for this activity.
- Extend your arms and stick in front of your body throughout this drill for better balance.
- Try to keep your eyes focused on a target area at the other end of the rink. Don't look down at your skates or the ice.
- Attempt to shoot your skates ahead quickly so that recovery under the body is possible.

(a)

(b)

(c)

33 SHOOT THE DUCK

Purpose

To reinforce proper edge control and balance points.

Procedure

1. As with the Russian Kip, players organize in waves with one group skating forward to gain momentum.
2. At the near blue line, players go into a sitting position and temporarily glide on both the flats of the skate edges.
3. Players then attempt to pull one leg off the ice while remaining in the sitting position and extend the leg directly in front of the body.
4. Players attempt to hold this position until they reach the other end of the rink.

Key Points

• This is another activity that will test your balance and leg strength.

• You should eventually be able to do this drill on either leg. As a progression for this activity you might alternate legs while in the sitting position.

• As with the Russian Kip, you should extend your arms and stick forward in front of your body to maximize balance.

• To avoid cheating on this drill, you must reach a full sitting position.

34 SWEDISH C-CUT, BACKWARD

Purpose

To use as a lead-up drill to reinforce the backward-skating stride.

Procedure

1. Players take positions anywhere around the rink 10 to 15 feet away from and facing the boards.
2. On the coach's whistle, all players use a single push from one leg to move toward the boards, then glide on the opposite skate (photo a).
3. The push skate must stay off the ice. Before reaching the boards players initiate a one-footed stop on the inside edge of the glide skate, keeping their weight over the ball of the foot (photo b).
4. Immediately upon stopping, players initiate a backward C-cut motion with the stop skate and attempt to glide backward to their starting location.

Key Points

- Place your weight on the ball of your glide foot.
- You must maintain sound knee and ankle bend to complete this drill successfully.
- Try to keep your upper body always over your glide skate.
- You must keep the initial push skate off the ice for the duration of this activity for it to be considered successful.
- As you complete the stop, you must snap the ankle joint to make the C-cut and propel you back to the starting position.

(a)

(b)

 RUSSIAN WALK

Purpose

To reinforce foot speed, quickness, and balance, and demonstrate the importance of upper-body posture in skating.

Procedure

1. Players form waves at one end of the rink as they did in the two previous drills.
2. A wave of players makes a single push to start momentum. They then drop to one knee so that both the knee and toe of the skate touch the ice (photo a).
3. Thereafter, players attempt to switch legs by transferring their weight from one skate to the other (photo b). They continue alternating their weight from one skate to the other as they travel the remaining distance of the ice surface (photo c).

Key Points

- It is vital that you keep your upper body straight with your head up and aligned over the glide, or support, leg.
- You will have to shift your upper-body position slightly from side to side as the support alternates from the left leg to the right leg.
- Your arms should be at your side with your stick in one hand only. Your arm movements will assist in maintaining your forward momentum. Move them front to back, not side to side.
- You must concentrate on touching both the knee and toe to the ice surface as you alternate legs. Do not cheat on this drill by going down only partway.
- As your balance improves, challenge yourself by alternating your legs more rapidly.

(a)

(b)

(c)

36 JUMP ROPE

Purpose

To develop better balance and improve conditioning.

Procedure

1. Players are in a wave formation at one end of the rink, each with a standard skipping rope. Players leave their sticks on the ice but keep their gloves on for safety.
2. On the whistle, players slowly move forward in their waves, skipping rope as they make their way down the ice (photo a).
3. The first waves may do only single-foot jumps. Ensuing waves can try the two-foot skipping technique (photo b).
4. As waves continue, the coach can arrange players in threesomes, with two players holding the rope while a third player attempts to skip.

Key Points

• You may find initially that you have trouble maintaining good balance because your weight moves either too far forward or backward on your skate edges.

• Don't be in a hurry at first. Work on maintaining a constant rhythm so that the actual skipping part becomes easier.

• Once you achieve a rhythm, don't look down. Instead, look forward at a target in the distance.

• You can try speed skipping as your skill improves, doubling the speed of the skipping rhythm. Try this first while stationary; then try it when in motion.

(a)

(b)

POWER PULLS

Purpose

To practice edge control and balance on one leg and to develop additional leg strength.

Procedure

1. Begin by standing at one end of the rink. Load your knees and give a powerful push with one leg toward the opposite end of the rink (photo a).
2. After pushing with one leg you should put your weight entirely on the opposite foot, making this the skate that contacts the ice. You must hold your initial push leg slightly off the ice surface the rest of the way down the ice (photo b).
3. By distributing your weight along the glide blade, continue to move in a snakelike fashion as far as you can without putting the other skate on the ice.
4. See if you can make it all the way to the other end by making C-cuts with your glide skate with both the inside and outside edges.
5. While moving forward, your weight distribution is on the heel. When skating backward, you should move your weight toward the balls of your feet.

Key Points

• If you cannot make it the entire distance, give yourself another push to get back on track.

• You will be successful if you learn to shift your body weight over the support, or glide, skate while making the C-cut, alternating from the inside edge to the outside edge.

• Focus on keeping your upper body quiet to help maintain speed.

(a)

(b)

Sample Practice Plans

To show you how to structure a practice using the activities in this book, we have provided some sample practice plans. When designing an effective practice session, coaches and players should first consider the following important factors.

Take Time to Prepare

Coaches should have a game plan for each practice session and share its objectives with the players. Most players want to improve and please their coaches. Players find this difficult, however, if they do not understand what the coach expects of them. Coaches should take the time to prepare and share their ideas before the team hits the ice.

Use the Entire Ice Surface Efficiently

Rather than running all full-ice drills, split the ice in halves, thirds, or even quarters as noted previously, depending on the theme for the day. Ice time is costly in many locations, so it is important to make every second count toward skill development.

Break the Team Into Workable Groups

To use ice time efficiently, organize practice so that players are active on the ice as much as possible. For example, a full-ice drill in which two players are active while 18 others stand motionless is rarely worthwhile. Break the team into smaller groups so that players can repeat each drill more often in the same amount of time.

Consider Station Work to Reinforce Specific Skills

Station-based learning is a popular concept in classrooms across North America, so why not try it on the ice as well? If the theme is individual skating skill improvement, divide the team into groups and place each at a specific drill station. You can adapt many of the drills in this book to work in stations.

The following practice plans combine drills described earlier. These three examples demonstrate how you can approach the topic of skating in a variety of ways with differing specific objectives. Although we have established these sessions as skating practices only, realize that it is easy to add pucks to many of the individual drills. Historically, if players came on the ice and saw that no pucks were present for the day's practice, mass panic would set in immediately! But having conducted many skating-only practices with players up to the professional level, we can guarantee that players will find the workouts interesting, challenging, and fun. An occasional session focused on skating skills is an effective way of adding variety to your practices while reinforcing important skating concepts that players might forget during the season. Intelligent repetition, a key to development in skating, is the concept that frames these practices.

You will notice in these lesson plans that we occasionally modify a drill from one part of the book to use in another skill area. We encourage you to be creative in designing your skating sessions. Players will enjoy the variety while the activities reinforce proper skills with proven techniques.

For the following practices, add at least 5 minutes for transition time between drills during a 50-minute session. Remember that most rinks allot 10 minutes each hour for resurfacing the ice. So of the 60-minute time slot typical for minor hockey, almost 15 minutes will be lost to organizational considerations. With this in mind we have provided approximately 45 minutes of drill time in each practice.

SAMPLE PRACTICE PLAN 1

Total Time: 60 minutes
Theme: Forward skating
Objective: To refine edge control and balance skills

Drill Sequence	Time Required (min)
1. **Begin with a warm-up sequence** *Designed to loosen muscles in preparation for practice*	6
2. **DRILL 1 — One-Legged Glide** *A simple activity to practice edge control using full-ice waves*	4
3. **DRILL 3 — Three-Count Recovery** *Reinforces upper-body positioning in another full-ice activity*	5
4. **DRILL 23 — Figure 8** *Develops edge control while incorporating glide turns*	5
5. **DRILL 15 — Falling Stick** *A fun partner drill that works on inside edge position off a V start*	3
6. **DRILL 24 — Slalom** *Move into groups and improve balance through edge control*	5
7. **DRILL 31 — Four Corners** *Remain in groups and try this pivoting activity*	5
8. **DRILL 36 — Jump Rope** *Bring out the ropes for a fun yet tiring series on the ice*	5
9. **Recap and finish with some form of game to conclude practice**	7

Total Activity Time	45

SAMPLE PRACTICE PLAN 2

Total Time: 60 minutes

Theme: Forward skating

Objective: To reinforce key turning skills in a stimulating environment

Drill Sequence	Time Required (min)

1. Begin with a warm-up sequence of your choice — 6

Designed to loosen muscles in preparation for practice

2. DRILL 6 — Frog Leaps — 5

Add a twist—after each leap players glide turn 90 degrees either left or right, then head up ice for another leap

3. DRILL 25 — Airplane — 5

Players now learn upper-body mechanics in a glide-turn drill

4. DRILL 16 — Sideways Walk — 5

Work on edge placement as a crossover lead-up

5. DRILL 28 — Sculling Circle — 5

A good motion drill to prepare for crossover turning

6. DRILL 27 — Partner Circle — 8

In pairs, players will enjoy a little competition while turning (remember to try this in both directions)

7. DRILL 18 — Zigzag — 5

Modify it so that players either glide or cross over at each pylon

8. Finish with a recap and game or scrimmage activity — 6

Total Activity Time   45

SAMPLE PRACTICE PLAN 3

Total Time: 60 minutes
Theme: Backward skating
Objective: To develop backward skating while enhancing player conditioning

Drill Sequence	Time Required (min)
1. **Begin with a warm-up sequence, done while skating backward**	6
2. **DRILL 7 — One-Legged Back Glide** *Players work on single-skate edge control*	4
3. **DRILL 8 — Backward Leg Load** *Reinforces the need for proper knee bend while skating backward*	4
4. **DRILL 22 — 360-Degree Turns** *Start out skating backward instead of forward*	4
5. **DRILL 10 — Alternate C-Cuts** *This will reinforce proper C-cut mechanics.*	5
6. **DRILL 21 — Partner Pull** *Turn around and try this drill with a partner going backward*	7
7. **DRILL 37 — Power Pulls** *See if you can do this backward the length of the ice*	5
8. **DRILL 32 — Russian Kip** *A drill that will test even the finest backward skaters*	5
9. **Recap key teaching points and finish with a game**	5

Total Activity Time	45

About Huron Hockey School

Hockey has improved dramatically over the past 27 years. Huron Hockey School, founded in 1970, has matched the sport's progression stride for stride as the leader in hockey instruction, both on the ice and in the classroom.

The Huron curriculum—annually updated, expanded, and now including a roller-hockey component—is used internationally from San Jose, California, to Saint John, New Brunswick, with 30 campuses in between, and includes resident schools in Traverse City, Michigan; Canton, New York; and Toronto, Ontario.

The seeds of Huron's dynamic growth can be traced to the hockey revolution that began in 1970, when Bobby Orr became the first defenseman in National Hockey League history to win the league scoring championship. While Orr's Boston Bruins went on to win the Stanley Cup Trophy that year, three young coaches realized the need for a more scientific approach to teaching the fundamentals of the sport they loved.

From the analytical minds of Ron Mason, now collegiate hockey's all-time leader in coaching wins, Bill Mahoney, former head coach of the Minnesota North Stars, and Brian Gilmour, an all-American at Boston University in 1967, evolved a now time-tested philosophy of hockey instruction by professional educators, people who know how to *teach* the game and know the nuances that make a hockey instructor effective. This concept of teaching hockey fundamentals has benefited more than 100,000 players, including over 350 who have made it to the National Hockey League.

Hockey has become a truly global sport, and Huron has become a global hockey school—one that prides itself on developing better players. International exchanges have taken Huron staff members to Russia, where in 1965, Mason studied under the legendary coach Anatoli Tarasov, the father of Soviet hockey. Today, the school regularly welcomes youngsters from Japan, Italy, Sweden, Finland, Holland, Denmark, Germany, Austria, and France, who all come to learn hockey the Huron way.

Paul O'Dacre
COO, Huron Hockey, Inc.

About the Authors

Coach Steve Cady has served as the top skating instructor for Huron Hockey School throughout the United States, Canada, and Europe for more than 20 years. A member of the NCAA Ice Hockey Rules Committee, for years Cady has been working with NHL players on their skating skills during the off-season. He's also conducted training sessions at the Olympic Development Centers in New York and Colorado. Cady lives in Oxford, Ohio.

K. Vern Stenlund, also one of the world's leading hockey instructors, has played professional hockey and coached the sport at all levels. He is also a consultant to Huron Hockey School, and has assisted in establishing satellite clinics in West Orange, NJ; Chicago and Geneva, IL; Toronto; Traverse City, MI; Ridgefield, CT; and Jackson, WY. Stenlund lives in Windsor, Ontario.

More hockey titles from Human Kinetics

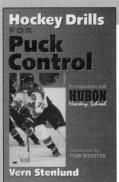
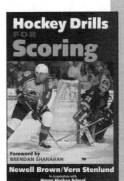
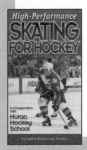